BEGINNING
PROGRAMMING
WITH ADA

BEGINNING PROGRAMMING WITH ADA

James A. Saxon, Ph.D.
Robert E. Fritz

PRENTICE-HALL, INC., Englewood Cliffs, New Jersey 07632

Library of Congress Cataloging in Publication Data

Saxon, James A.
    Beginning programming with Ada.

    Includes index.
    1. Ada (Computer program language) I. Fritz,
Robert E. II. Title.
QA76.73.A35S28 1983   001.64'24   82-24997
ISBN 0-13-071688-X

Editorial/production supervision: *Lynn Frankel*
Art production: *Frances M. Kasturas*
Cover design: *Photo Plus Art*(**Celine Brandes**)
Manufacturing buyer: *Gordon Osbourne*

Printed in the United States of America

10 9 8 7 6 5 4 3 2 1

ISBN 0-13-071688-X

Prentice-Hall International, Inc., *London*
Prentice-Hall of Australia Pty. Limited, *Sydney*
Editora Prentice-Hall do Brasil, Ltda., *Rio de Janeiro*
Prentice-Hall Canada Inc., *Toronto*
Prentice-Hall of India Private Limited, *New Delhi*
Prentice-Hall of Japan, Inc., *Tokyo*
Prentice-Hall of Southeast Asia Pte. Ltd., *Singapore*
Whitehall Books Limited, *Wellington, New Zealand*

The function of a teacher [or author of teaching books] is to transform the difficult topic into simple, easy to understand, units of instruction. He should not concern himself with methods and terminology aimed solely at enhancing his reputation for erudite expression. It is hoped that this text lives up to these principles.

The Authors

CONTENTS

Contents continued

Contents continued

Contents continued

PREFACE

Background

The high level programming language called Ada is the result of a large scale collective effort to design a language with a great deal of expressive power covering a wide range of applications. The effort was instituted and supported by the Department of Defense (DoD) because of the proliferation of languages throughout the Department.

The need for a language that could replace many languages throughout DoD was felt to be both a money saving and a time saving effort. Studies showed that savings could be as high as 10 to 20 billion dollars. Developmental efforts began in 1975 and have continued year after year. Undoubtedly, changes and improvements will continue to be made as the language is used by an increasing number of programmers.

High level languages for the 60's were FORTRAN, COBOL, PL/1, JOVIAL and CMS–2. These languages are still very much in use today. In the early 70's a new language, PASCAL, was developed and swept the country by storm. It may be considered to be the transition language to Ada since PASCAL was the base language used in the development of Ada.

Just as FORTRAN was considered to be the language of the 60's and PASCAL the language of the 70's, Ada should become the language of the 80's and possibly the 90's.

Historical Note

To understand why the language was called Ada, a brief history of Charles Babbage must be covered. Babbage was born in Devonshire, England in 1792, the son of a banker from whom he inherited a large private income. He was the first man with a clear conception of modern day computing, but he was a hundred years ahead of his time because the technology of his day was just not up to his visionary dreams.

He developed a machine, called the Difference Engine, on which the first error-free life tables were produced for the use of insurance companies. The first "difference engine" used in this country was a Burroughs accounting machine introduced in 1913.

Babbage developed a method of analysis, today known as Operations Research. With this method [the study of facts, rather than using just reasoning, which could be unsound], he analyzed the pin-making industry, the printing trade and the Post Office, among other industries. He showed conclusively that it would be more reasonable and economical to charge a flat fee for postage without regard to the distance the mail must travel. He devised the method of identifying lighthouses by occulting their lights. He proposed a method of reading the annual rings of trees to recognize cycles of wet and dry weather. This method was rediscovered 50 years later.

The above is just a small list of his many accomplishments, but Babbage is best known for his Analytic Engine, which was in nearly every respect precisely what modern day computers became a hundred years later. His input and output was to be punched cards [invented for controlling looms for weaving by M. Jacquard]. What we presently call the arithmetic and logic unit, he called the mill and the modern day term memory, he called the store [the terms storage and memory are interchangeable today]. A block diagram of the Analytic Engine is shown below.

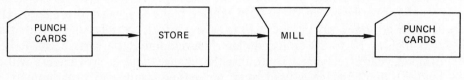

Fig. 1 — Analytic Engine

Simplified block diagram of a computer. The resemblance is obvious.

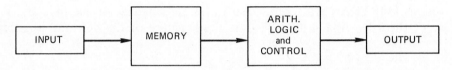

Fig. 2 — Simplified Diagram of a Computer

In 1840, Babbage gave a series of lectures in Turin, Italy. The lectures were attended by Menabrea, who was so impressed that he wrote an account of the lectures. The paper was translated into English by Ada Augusta, the Countess of Lovelace [the only daughter of the famous poet, Lord Byron].

Ada was a mathematician, who studied for many years under DeMorgan. She was a frequent visitor to Babbage's shop and understood his theories of the Difference and Analytic Engines quite well. She added greatly to Menabrea's account during her translation by including comprehensive notes about the Engine and a series of examples of its use, including a program for computing Bernoulli numbers by a very sophisticated method. This program can be considered to be the first computer program ever devised and Ada, therefore, became the first programmer. This language was named in her honor.

Purpose and Scope

The purpose of this manual is to teach the Ada high-level language to beginning programmers. The text will cover the language using simple, straightforward explanations, examples and problems so that the student will progress through actual work with each facet of language development.

While the primary goal of the book is to teach beginning programmers the fundamentals of programming, the secondary goals will be to teach the fundamentals of software development in a large system environment. In this context, the term software refers to the program that instructs the computer in its operation.

It is hoped that the text will lead the programmer to the knowledge that writing a program is just one stage of the software life cycle, and that there are responsibilities to the future users and maintainers of the software. Just as the software system designer must pass sufficient information to the programmer for him to write the program, so too must the programmer document his efforts for those who will use or modify his program.

This book was prepared with consideration for the ACM [Association for Computing Machinery] curricula for computer science courses and meets many of the standards set for the CS1 [Computer Science 1] course.[1] However, a more object-oriented approach is taken to algorithm design and development because it is felt that Ada gives more power in this area.

Chapter 1 is included as a very brief introduction to the concepts and terminology of data processing. Students who have had an introductory course in this subject area may skip this chapter.

How to Use this Text

This text has been developed to teach the beginner the fundamentals of programming in the Ada language.

The format used in a teaching text is quite different from that of a reference manual for experienced programmers. This text is designed for use as a teaching instrument only.

There are large numbers of problems and exercises scattered throughout the manual. In every case, the correct answer is given on the back of the problem page. The student is to work each problem on scratch paper. The answer is then checked against the correct answer. If the answer given by the student is incorrect, the previous pages should be reviewed. There is nothing to keep the student from looking at the correct answer before attempting to work the problem except the realization that he will not learn to program if he does this.

This text should facilitate the teaching of Ada to college students since the material to be learned is broken down into small, logically sequential steps which lead [with the aid of many examples and problems] to the fundamental knowledges necessary in the programming of problem solutions with Ada.

---

[1] R. H. Austing, B. H. Barnes, D. T. Bonnette, G.E.Engel, G. Stokes, Eds.: Curriculum '78: Recommendations for the Undergraduate Program in Computer Science. Communications of the Association for Computing Machinery, V. 22, No. 3, March 1979, pp. 147–166.

Acknowledgements

The technical assistance given by Mr. Herbert Mayer, Staff Engineer, Burroughs Corporation, San Diego, California, in the careful review and thoughtful comments provided is gratefully acknowledged by the authors. Special thanks must also go to Susann M. Johnston for the care and precision with which she typed the original manuscript.

BEGINNING PROGRAMMING WITH ADA

1

INTRODUCTION
TO
DATA PROCESSING

INTRODUCTION TO DATA PROCESSING

A. The Processing Cycle

Every data-processing application follows a basic processing cycle. That is, each job or application will adhere to three basic steps, no matter how large or small the job may be. The three steps are input, processing, and output. This cycle can be expressed in symbolic form as follows:

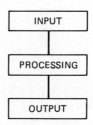

Irrespective of the method used to process data, this cycle will be followed.

B. The Language of the Computer

It takes little more than a casual observation to be aware that data is universal and is created in immeasurable quantities. Also, the sources of data are widespread and divergent, ranging all the way from the sale of a licorice stick in a candy store to a seismographic reading of an underground atomic blast.

For the present, attention will be directed between these two extremes, with a look at the sources of business data. Data originates with business activity. Goods are sold, purchased, ordered, received, moved, manufactured, and destroyed. Men are hired, fired, promoted, classified, reclassified, assigned, reassigned, paid, and retired. Money is received, paid out, loaned, borrowed, lost, and stolen. As each activity takes place, it creates data with potential importance to record and process.

The original recording of a business transaction is done on a source document. Source documents take the names of that which they record. Sales orders record a sale, material receiving reports record the receipt of merchandise or materials, etc.

Source documents are then the evidence of data for processing. They are the written documents from which the processing cycle begins. They are written in conventional language for human understanding. If, however, the data is to be processed by machine, a secondary recording of the data must usually be made in a machine-readable language or code. Today, computers are not yet smart enough to always read and understand text meant for the human eye, but there is great potential for this in the future.

C. Computer Capabilities and Limitations

A computer can perform repetitive operations hundreds, thousands, or millions of times without getting tired or careless. It never gets bored with an operation; therefore, it never creates errors that would be normal for a human being under similar conditions.

A computer can be designed to be as flexible or specialized as desired. It can be designed to be a special-purpose computer to solve only a specific type of problem, or it can be designed to be a general-purpose computer which will solve many types of problems. There is a further breakdown even within the general-purpose computer class in that it may be specifically designed to serve as a scientific computer or as a business applications computer.

The computer can provide answers that are as accurate as desired, and it has the capability of checking itself to doubly assure accuracy of results.

The biggest computer limitation is that it cannot do anything that it is not ordered to do. It does its work exactly as it has been directed, making no independent judgments. It cannot assimilate new facts that have not been fed to it, and it does not have the capability of performing any creative activity. The one thing that it can do is to follow orders, and this it does marvelously well.

The humans who arrange the work for the computers and who translate the work into language of a type which the machines are engineered to accommodate are called programmers. The instructions that they write are called programs.

Although a computer gives the impression that it is extremely flexible and can do a vast variety of jobs, one of its major limitations is its inflexibility. Programming a problem may cost so much expended effort in both time and money that it may be impractical to make serious changes after the program has been completed.

It must also be understood that, although the computer appears to solve monumentally difficult problems, in reality it performs only basic arithmetic. Therefore, a difficult mathematical problem must be broken down into simple step-by-step procedures, which may become a most laborious and time-consuming chore for the programmer.

In spite of the fact that computers work at fantastic speeds, there are certain applications for which the process is still not fast enough. In these areas, particularly in real-time situations, solutions and answers are required in seconds and the computer may take hours to achieve the desired results.

These limitations, although slightly exaggerated, are very real and will not be overcome until a low-cost, lightweight, extremely reliable digital computer is developed that will have the capability of providing instantaneous response without previous programming effort. It is not often understood by the layman that months, and even years, of programming effort have preceded the simple ease with which a computer accomplishes its given tasks.

In the final analysis, a digital computer is simply an arithmetic machine that receives individual digits, performs simple arithmetic, and produces answers consisting of individual digits. Special techniques can change the digits to alphabetic characters, but the computer handles all of its information simply as digits.

D. Computer Hardware

1. Basic Components

All digital computers are composed of the following five major components: [1] input devices, [2] memory unit, [3] control unit, [4] arithmetic unit, and [5] output devices. The block diagram below shows the interrelationships of these components.

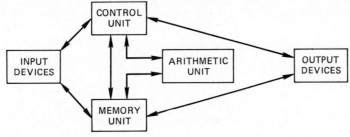

The arithmetic unit carries out the arithmetic calculations. It is the operational portion of the computer, performing the actual work of calculation and comparison.

The work of the arithmetic unit must be controlled so that it will accomplish the desired tasks. The control unit carries out this requirement. It is the switching section of the computer, receiving incoming information and deciding what to do and when to do it. It also decides what to do with the results, and it controls the work of the arithmetic unit.

The memory unit [also referred to as the storage unit] performs the function of storing information until it is needed by one of the other components of the system. It provides information to both the airthmetic and control units. Although there are many types of memory units, they all perform the function of holding information until it is required.

Finally, input devices are used for people to communicate with the computer so that it will know what should be accomplished, and output devices are used to communicate with people regarding the results of the computer calculations.

These statements are highly generalized, of course, but the actual internal operation of the computer itself [the control, memory, and arithmetic units] is not usually of major concern to computer users. The details of wiring and methods of switching used are only of concern to the maintenance technician and the design engineer.

2. Primary Storage

The three blocks in the figure above labeled memory, control and arithmetic are contained in the Central Processing Unit (CPU) of the computer. Storage is often used as an alternate term to memory since this portion of the computer literally stores information in the form of bits [ones and zeros] and retains the information in readily accessible form until it is needed.

There are many types of storage devices and more types are constantly being developed in an attempt to make storage more compact and less expensive. Some storage devices are:

Magnetic Disk	Thin Film
Magnetic Tape	Magnetic Core
	Semiconductor

When reference is made to primary storage, the reference is to storage which is an integral part of the CPU, such as magnetic core or semiconductor storage. Other storage devices also serve as input and output media.

There are two important terms to learn in connection with storage devices: [1] access time refers to the speed with which stored data can be extracted from the storage device, and [2] capacity refers to the maximum amount of data that can be stored.

Access time is determined by the particular storage device. In magnetic core storage or semiconductor storage devices, equal amounts of time is required to access any group of stored bits. Main storage systems are called random access systems since any item can be selected for extraction and the data is available in the same amount of time [faster than a millionth of a second] that it takes for data extraction of any other item.

3. The Stored Program

The ability to store large amounts of data is not the only function of the storage unit. The data referred to here is that which the computer will use in its calculations. Even more important is the fact that the program that instructs the computer in its functions is contained within the storage [or memory] unit.

A stored program system, then, is one that stores its instructions internally. A sequence of instructions to solve a problem is called a program. The individual instructions are called program steps.   The program is converted from writing to the language understandable to the computer [machine language] and it is then loaded into the computer [i.e., placed into the memory unit of the computer]. When data is fed into the computer, the stored program acts on the data to produce the desired results.

4. Secondary Storage

Any storage device not contained within the CPU of the computer is called a secondary storage device. Some of the devices are used to supplement the memory unit of the computer, others are used as input-output devices and still others can serve a dual function of increasing the effective memory of the computer and permitting the use of the device as an input or output medium.

The most commonly used secondary storage device is the magnetic disk. It has the capability of adding a fantastic amount of memory to the computer. The disk may remain permanently in its cabinet connected directly to computer memory or it may be packaged in portable disk packs which may be removed and stored when not in use. The fixed disks are usually used to store systems programs and often used programs, while the removable disk packs are used for less frequently used programs.

Disk packs are constructed much like the coin operated phonographs [jukeboxes]. Access to the disk surfaces is provided by read-write heads on both sides, like the two sides of a phonograph record.

As an example, a disk unit may have four drives [or modules] with a single drive containing 10 disks. Each disk has two surfaces with 100 tracks [concentric rings] on each surface. Each track is divided into 20 sectors, with a storage capacity of 200 characters per sector. This totals 32 million characters for the disk unit. There are some disk units that hold upward of a half billion characters.

5. Input-Output (I/O) Devices

There is a nearly limitless list of I/O devices. The magnetic disk mentioned above is but one of them. In the earlier days of computing, the punched card was the major instrument of input and output. Although punched cards are still used in many installations, they have been replaced to a large extent by the diskette [also known as "floppy disk"] because it is much faster to handle, simpler to use and much less bulky [one diskette will hold as much information as 2000 punch cards].

A few commonly used I/O devices are mentioned below.

Paper Tape	—Round holes are punched in paper tape to represent alpha and numeric characters. May have 5 to 8 channels. Reads at 150 to 2000 characters per second.
Magnetic Tape	—Tape is 2400 feet long and moves at approximately 200 inches per second. Can hold up to 40 million characters [about 500,000 punch cards] and can be written at speeds of 15,000 to 800,000 cps.
Printer	—Up to 220 positions per line of print. Many different types including print wheel, wire matrix, chain, bar and [now] laser. Printing speeds are from 400 lines per minute to 1200 lines per minute. Laser printers achieve speeds of 6,000 to 15,000 lines per minute.

Cathode Ray Tube	—Like the familiar TV screen [which is in fact a CRT]. The face of the tube is laid out in a grid pattern, the display area can be from 200 to 2000 characters. When power is turned on, the grid matrix shows dots of low potential [not visible]. Information is fed in as binary 1's and 0's and the 1's are <u>registered,</u> causing the dot to be surrounded by a circle, raising the potential and making it visible. Data is written on the screen up to 240 cps. Transmission speeds vary from 10 to 10,000 cps.
Magnetic Ink Character Recognition	—Reads the precoded material on a check [identifies the bank and the account number of the individual], thus allowing the speedy processing of millions of checks monthly. The reader can process 150 to 2000 checks a minute. As far back as 1976, the banking industry was processing 24 billion checks a year and the volume expected to double every two to three years. Without these machines [and computers] it would not now be possible for the banking industry to function with checking accounts for its clients.
Optical Character Recognition	—This technique makes it possible to read from printed documents. It also does <u>mark</u> reading of pen and pencil marks. These marks placed in special places on a document, represent specific information that can be processed by the computer.
Microfilm Output	—In spite of its speed, there are times when printouts from the computer are too slow. It is possible to place information on magnetic tape, then feed it to a Computer On Microfilm (COM) recorder which flashes information in page form on a CRT for a fraction of a second. It is recorded by ultra high speed camera. The exposed microfilm is automatically processed and duplicated. The storage reduction of information is fantastic. For example, a room full of paper [10 x 10 x 10 feet in size] can be stored in a single file 8 x 4 x 6 inches in size.

E. <u>Elementary Programming</u>

1. Bits, Words, Characters and Bytes

     The word bit is an abbreviation of <u>binary digit</u>, the base-2 system component in either the "on" or the "off" condition. A specified number of bits comprise a computer word, which is treated by the circuitry as a unit and transferred as such. A word in a <u>fixed-word-length</u> machine is made up of bits, and characters can be represented in the words, but every word is exactly as long as every other word in this type of machine. The size of the word varies with different machines, but the basic principle is the same. A unit of information is represented by a fixed-length word. A word may be 16 bits long, 32 bits, 64 bits, or any other arbitrary number established by the designers. On most machines, a word must start on definite bit boundaries, which are an integral multiple of the word size; this is called 'ALIGNMENT'.

Example:

A 32-bit word in a fixed-word-length machine would look [symbolically] something like this:

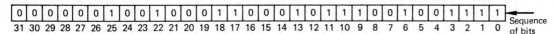

| 0 | 0 | 0 | 0 | 0 | 0 | 1 | 0 | 0 | 1 | 0 | 0 | 0 | 1 | 1 | 0 | 0 | 0 | 1 | 0 | 1 | 1 | 1 | 0 | 0 | 1 | 0 | 0 | 1 | 1 | 1 | 1 |
31 30 29 28 27 26 25 24 23 22 21 20 19 18 17 16 15 14 13 12 11 10 9 8 7 6 5 4 3 2 1 0

Sequence of bits

If it takes eight <u>bits</u> to represent a digit, four digits would fit into this word.

If it takes eight bits to make up one character, then a 16-bit word would contain two characters to a word and a 64-bit word would contain eight characters to a word.

A <u>byte</u> consists of eight bits in consecutive sequence. Bytes are successive and do not overlap each other in computer memory.

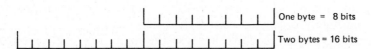

One byte = 8 bits

Two bytes = 16 bits

The basic unit that can be directly referenced by the programmer is called a <u>word</u>. A word is usually some multiple of a byte and the size of the word varies with the computer being used. Some computers allow the programmer to reference <u>half-word</u>, <u>double-word</u>, or even <u>byte</u> or <u>bits.</u>

When working with a lower level language than Ada, the programmer must know what the word size is and what may be referenced in the particular computer.

2. Computer Instructions

Computer instructions are the building blocks of a computer program. They fall into the following three broad classifications:

   a. <u>Transfer</u> of information from one storage location or medium to another.

   b. <u>Arithmetic</u> manipulation.

   c. <u>Decisions</u> on which path to follow, based upon comparisons, magnitude of numbers, specific keys, etc.

To develop a computer program, the three types of operations listed above are combined in various ways to solve a particular problem. <u>Coding</u> is the term used for translating the program into the instructions of a specific computer.

3. Execution Sequence

Instructions are carried out by the computer in the sequence of storage addresses in which they are located. The control unit has an instruction counter which keeps track of the location of the instruction being executed and the one that will follow. If an instruction specifically calls for a change in the sequence, this change will be followed, either to branch ahead or to branch back to a previous part of the program. Otherwise the instructions will be executed one after the other until the end of the program is reached. The logical end of the program is only sometimes the same as the physical end of the program.

4. Structured Programming

One of the newer approaches to programming is called <u>structured</u> programming. This term refers to a particular type of program structure and is somewhat misleading in that a program could be well-designed and have structure without following the rules of a "structured program." Conversely, a "formally structured program" may be utterly useless and chaotic.

A structured program in the narrowest sense is one containing only the following basic logic structures:

    a. SEQUENCE   A sequence of two or more operations.
    b. IFTHENELSE   The conditional execution of one of two operations.
    c. DO WHILE   The repetition of an operation while the condition is true.

An additional characteristic is that each of the three operations has only one entry at the top and one exit at the bottom. Unconditional branches [such as GO TO's] are avoided in structured programming because they often lead to multiple exits from a single programming sequence.

The proponents of structured programming offer the following advantages:

    a. Programs can be written more quickly and will be more error-free because a highly organized approach is necessary.
    b. Programs are more readable because the logic flow is always from the top down; branching around is eliminated.
    c. Programs can be modified more readily.

Another valid reason for the use of structured programming is that the technique is endorsed by the Department of Defense (DOD).

5. Programming Languages and Compilers

Compiled languages are generally referred to as high level languages because they are more English-like or mathematically oriented than low level languages [such as machine or assembly languages].

The program that changes the higher level language into machine language is called a compiler. A single statement in such a language may cause the generation of a whole group of instructions and this is where it differs from the lower level languages, in which one symbolic instruction causes the generation of one machine language instruction.

The group of instructions written by the programmer is called the source program. This is translated into machine language by the compiler. The translated program [called the object program] can then be run on the computer.

Although each different type of computer must have its own compiler, the source program written in Ada [or any other high-level, strictly standardized language] should not have to be rewritten to run on different computers. Usually only minor modifications are required plus a recompilation of the source program to the object language of the other computer.

Computer programs [such as compilers or programs to solve problems] are generally termed software as opposed to hardware [which refers to actual computer equipment]. In the past few years software has become almost more important than hardware and manufacturers vie with each other to produce more and more sophisticated software packages to help sell their hardware.

6. Operating System Programs

The function of the operating system (OS) is to perform the many housekeeping duties necessary in the overall operation of the system [such as loading and unloading input and output equipment, clearing CPU storage between jobs, organizing the sequence of jobs to be processed, loading in the next job as one job is finished and a multitude of other minor duties]. The portion of the OS that controls the input and output devices is called the IOCS (Input/Output Control System).

Modern computer facilities could not operate without efficient operating systems. One of the major functions of the OS is to keep the computer running with a minimum of idle time and in the most efficient manner possible.

The OS is also concerned with the economical handling of <u>multiprogramming</u>, which is the method of concurrent execution of two or more different programs by a single computer during relatively the same time span. The way this works is that there are a number of programs stored in memory or in handily available storage and that the computer executes a portion of one program, then a portion of another, the switch being made almost instantaneously. Since the CPU works much faster than the input/output (I/O) devices, the computer does not have to remain idle while one program is bringing in data or sending out data.

With multiprogramming, it is possible for several users to share the time of the computer [timesharing], but the work of the OS becomes more and more complicated. Operating systems have become collections of master control and processing programs that control the scheduling, loading and program call-up functions of the computer.

F. Numbering Systems

1. Binary Numbering System

Counting on the fingers has a definite bearing on the method of counting for computers. Since the fingers are a basic counting device, every principle that applies to the fingers also applies to more sophisticated counting devices. It can be mathematically proven that the most efficient code that can be developed for the fingers is one that doubles the value of each finger.

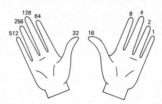

This code is often called the 8—4—2—1 code after the four lowest numbers in the sequence. This code can be used to count from zero to a maximum of 1,023. Including the zero, 1024 values can be represented.

$$512+256+128+64+32+16+8+4+2+1=1,023$$

Modern digital computers also use the 8—4—2—1 code. Nearly all computers work in the binary mode. This is a base-2 system utilizing only two digits, zero and one. This is most convenient for computers because an electrical field may be "on" or "off" and a magnetic device may be magnetized or not magnetized. These are also base-2 types of actions. Since computers use binary circuits, the internal arithmetic of computers is binary in nature.

The importance of numbering systems other than decimal is not immediately apparent to most people. We are so accustomed to using the decimal system that it has become almost second nature to us, while other numbering systems seem strange and difficult. They are difficult only because they are strange.

Binary and Octal Numbering Systems courtesy of <u>Basic Principles of Data Processing.</u> Saxon and Steyer, Prentice—Hall, Inc. 1970.

In the binary system, only two digits are used, zero and one. It requires the invention of a code [using only zero and one] that will cover all possible combinations of numbers to have a workable system. An arbitrary code could easily be devised, but we want a very efficient code and for this reason the 8—4—2—1 code will be utilized. Details of this code and some of the methods for using it will be covered in the following pages.

a. Counting in the binary system

The 8—4—2—1 code described on the previous page is, in fact, the binary code. It utilizes just two digits, zero and one. In such a two-state code, the one is arbitrarily chosen as the on condition and the zero as the off condition. Therefore, only the ones will be counted in a sequence of binary numbers.

The location of each of the ones [based on the 8—4—2—1 code] is the key to its value, as shown in the table below.

Code value →	512	256	128	64	32	16	8	4	2	1	Count only ones
	0	0	0	0	0	1	0	1	0	0	= 20 (16 + 4)
	0	0	0	0	1	0	0	1	0	1	= 37 (32 + 4 + 1)
	0	0	0	0	0	1	1	0	1	1	= 27 (16 + 8 + 2 + 1)

Code values of the 8—4—2—1 code

It is important to note that the values given to each binary position start from the right and progress to the left. [If this sequence were reversed, the results would be entirely different.] The rightmost position, then, is the position of the least-significant digit (LSD) and the leftmost position is that of the most-significant digit (MSD). Notice that this is exactly the same as in the decimal numbering system, in which the leftmost position is the most significant.

A number of other codes based on the binary system are possible, and many such codes are used for computers. The 8—4—2—1 code described above is usually called the pure binary code.

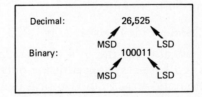

Position Significance of Numbers

b. Binary compared to decimal

Since binary numbers tend to be extremely long [roughly 3.3 times longer than their equivalent decimal numbers], it is more convenient to group them in threes. This does not change the relative value of each position but simply makes it easier to read.

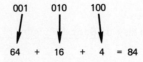

Counting in the binary system is as follows:

Decimal	Binary	Decimal	Binary
0	000	5	101
1	001	6	110
2	010	7	111
3	011	8	001 000
4	100	9	001 001

Since the binary system only contains 0 and 1, it is necessary to take the same "move" at 2 that is taken at 10 in the decimal system. This is to place a "1" to the left and start again [at the right] with "0." Therefore, a decimal 2 is a binary 10, 3 is 11, and then another shift must be made, adding 1 to the left and starting again with 0.

Examples

Convert the following decimal numbers to binary:

1. In the 8—4—2—1 sequence, on the preceding page, find the number just less than the value of the one to be converted. Start with this number, and continue adding until the required number is reached.

$$22=010 \quad 110$$

$$16+4+2=22$$

2. Add zeros to the left of the MSD to complete this last [leftmost] group of three binary digits.

$$76=001 \quad 001 \quad 100$$

$$64+8+4=76$$

2. Octal Numbering System

We have said that the binary system is a base-2 system. The octal numbering system is a base-8 system and is very convenient to use as a shorthand to binary.

Since it is a base-8 system, it will utilize only the numerals 0 through 7. Counting in this system is as shown below [notice that 8 and 9 are never used]:

Decimal	Octal	Decimal	Octal
0	0	8	10
1	1	9	11
2	2	10	12
3	3	11	13
4	4	12	14
5	5	13	15
6	6	14	16
7	7	15	17

Decimal to octal conversion.

When writing a number in octal, it is usual to designate the system in the following manner: 376_8. The subscript 8 indicates that 376 is an octal number.

As in the decimal and binary systems, the value of each digit in a sequence of numbers is definitely fixed.

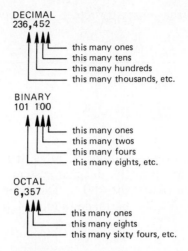

DECIMAL
236,452

— this many ones
— this many tens
— this many hundreds
— this many thousands, etc.

BINARY
101 100

— this many ones
— this many twos
— this many fours
— this many eights, etc.

OCTAL
6,357

— this many ones
— this many eights
— this many sixty fours, etc.

a. Conversion between octal and binary

    The relationship between octal and binary is so simple that conversion may be made instantaneously. Consider every binary number in groups of threes [001010101=001 010 101]. Now, each grouping of three binary digits is identified by ones, twos, and fours positions, and these are used to convert to octal.

Fours	Twos	Ones	Fours	Twos	Ones	Fours	Twos	Ones
0	0	1	0	1	0	1	0	1

Octal   1   Octal   2   Octal   5

Conversely, each octal number is converted to three binary numbers as shown below. The binary representation of the octal numbers is often called binary-coded octal.

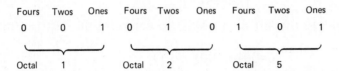

$$3 \quad 7 \quad 6 \quad 5_8$$

Binary: 011   111   110   101

Octal to binary conversion

Octal	Binary
1	001
2	010
3	011
4	100
5	101
6	110
7	111

b. Converting from octal to decimal

    This is usually accomplished by looking up the number in a conversion table. It may be accomplished manually in the following manner:
    Multiply each octal position in turn by eight, starting with the leftmost position. Then add the next number to the result, multiplying the sum by eight, and continue until the last digit is reached. This one is not to be multiplied.

Examples

1.

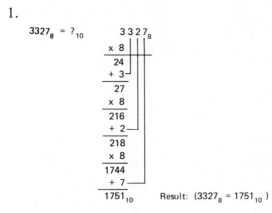

$3327_8 = ?_{10}$

$$
\begin{array}{r}
3\,3\,2\,7_8 \\
\times\ 8 \\
\hline
24 \\
+\ 3 \\
\hline
27 \\
\times\ 8 \\
\hline
216 \\
+\ 2 \\
\hline
218 \\
\times\ 8 \\
\hline
1744 \\
+\ 7 \\
\hline
1751_{10}
\end{array}
$$

Result: $(3327_8 = 1751_{10})$

2.

$426_8 = ?_{10}$

$$
\begin{array}{r}
4\,2\,6_8 \\
\times\ 8 \\
\hline
32 \\
+\ 2 \\
\hline
34 \\
\times\ 8 \\
\hline
272 \\
+\ 6 \\
\hline
278_{10}
\end{array}
$$

Result: $(426_8 = 278_{10})$

c. Converting from decimal to octal

This procedure is also generally accomplished by checking a conversion table, but it may be done manually in the following manner:

Successively divide the decimal figure by eight, until no further division is possible. The octal result will be the last quotient figure, followed by each of the remainders, starting from the last and finishing with the first.

Examples

1.

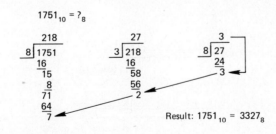

$1751_{10} = ?_8$

Result: $1751_{10} = 3327_8$

13

2.

$$278_{10} = ?_8$$

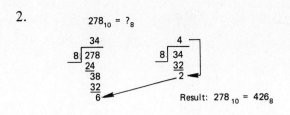

Result: $278_{10} = 426_8$

- -

3.

$$15273_{10} = ?_8$$

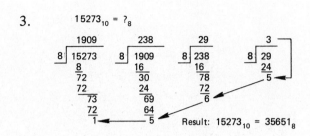

Result: $15273_{10} = 35651_8$

3. Hexadecimal Numbering System

The hexadecimal system is a base-16 system. The decimal digits 0 through 9 are used as the first 10 digits [just as in the decimal system], followed by the letters A through F, which represent the values of 10, 11, 12, 13, 14 and 15.

In the hexadecimal system, four binary characters [bits] make up a recognizable character. It may be thought of as half of a byte. Two hexadecimal digits make up one byte, the rightmost four bits constituting one hexadecimal digit and the leftmost four bits constituting another hexadecimal digit.

Examples

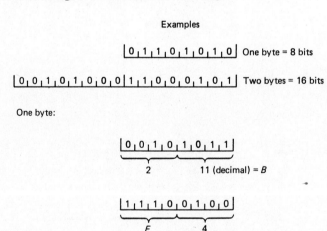

There is a little translation involved here. First, the bits must be translated to their decimal equivalents, then [if it is above 9] a second translation to hexadecimal must be made.

The numbering systems discussed to this point [binary, octal and hexadecimal] are the most important to the study of programming, but Ada will allow the use of any numbering system up to and including base 16.

14

The symbols used in bases 2 through 16 are shown below:

Symbols Used in Ada

Base		Symbols or Digits
2	[binary]	0 1
3		0 1 2
4		0 1 2 3
5		0 1 2 3 4
6		0 1 2 3 4 5
7		0 1 2 3 4 5 6
8	[octal]	0 1 2 3 4 5 6 7
9		0 1 2 3 4 5 6 7 8
10	[decimal]	0 1 2 3 4 5 6 7 8 9
11		0 1 2 3 4 5 6 7 8 9 A
12		0 1 2 3 4 5 6 7 8 9 A B
13		0 1 2 3 4 5 6 7 8 9 A B C
14		0 1 2 3 4 5 6 7 8 9 A B C D
15		0 1 2 3 4 5 6 7 8 9 A B C D E
16	[hexadecimal]	0 1 2 3 4 5 6 7 8 9 A B C D E F

Comparison of some number bases — representation in:

decimal	binary	octal	hexadecimal
0	0000 0000	000	00
1	0000 0001	001	01
2	0000 0010	002	02
3	0000 0011	003	03
4	0000 0100	004	04
7	0000 0111	007	07
8	0000 1000	010	08
10	0000 1010	012	0A
15	0000 1111	017	0F
16	0001 0000	020	10
25	0001 1001	031	19

G. Computer Systems

1. Historical Development

The historical development of computing is one of large gains over short periods of time. Development can be measured in generations of approximately five years each.

1st generation — starting approximately in 1955 for the early business computers, consisting of vacuum tube systems.

2nd generation — approximately 1960 — vacuum tubes were replaced by transistors.

3rd generation — 1965 — integrated circuits (IC) with logical components on a single chip:
  a. small scale — 4 components
  b. medium scale — 10 to 20 components
  c. start of large scale — up to 100 components

4th generation — 1970 — large scale integration (LSI). Up to 20,000 components on a chip 1/4" x 1/4" in size.

5th generation — 1975 — 40 to 60,000 components on a single chip.

6th generation — 1980 — laser technology, electronic funds transfer (EFT).

Each generation showed an increase in speed and a decrease in the size of the equipment until the speed of operation is nearing the speed of light and size is becoming so tiny that it borders on the incredible.

2. Types of Systems

Computer systems can be classified into three major types: [1] large-scale systems, [2] medium-scale systems and [3] small-scale systems. Each of these types has its own place in the overall scheme of data processing.

Size differences between various computers are rather difficult to describe, but basically the differences are expressed in the size of memory and the speed of execution. Other methods of comparison between various computer systems are the cost factor and the type of work the computer is expected to accomplish.

Perhaps the simplest way to show the differences is by means of a comparative table, keeping in mind that the low end of each category overlaps the high end of the next category.

Table Comparing Computer Systems*

| TYPE | COST | MEMORY | | NUMBER OF REGISTERS | INSTRUC-TIONS |
		WORD SIZE	SPEED		
Super Computer	7 million [only a very few] Weather Bureau Bureau of Standards	64 bit word	50 nanoseconds	520	All have large sets of instructions from 150 to several hundred
Large scale	1 million	32, 48 [multiples of 8]	500 nanosec. to 250 nanosec.	64	
Medium scale	1/4 to 1/2 million [peripherals are quite costly]	32 bits [4 bytes]	500–750 nanosec.	32	
Mini	bottom—6 – 8 thousand top—60 to 80 thousand	16 bits [2 bytes]	750 microsec. to 1000 nanosec.	16	can do floating pt. arithmetic
Micro	$1,000 – and down	8 bits [1 byte]	1 – 2 microsec.	4	approx. 80 with mply. and divide

*The figures in this table are approximations and are not meant to be precise.

16

The large and medium scale computers are the ones most generally thought of when computing is discussed, but the mini and the micro are becoming more and more useful because of their adaptability and the reasonableness of the acquisition cost.

3. Minicomputers

A minicomputer is a small sized general purpose computer doing the same things that the large computers do. The major difference is that they have limited capability to process data because:

        a. core memory is small
        b. word size is small
        c. arithmetic capability is limited
        d. software is limited
        e. I/O is good, but also limited

The major uses at this time are:

[1] Laboratory applications [25%] where a mini is dedicated to a particular process, or a series of minis that control parts of a complex application,

[2] numerical control of machine tools and other machines [40%] including teleprocessing and other industrial applications and

[3] business systems, educational systems and various miscellaneous systems comprise the remaining 35% of the field.

4. Microcomputers

The micro is a direct descendent of the mini. The difference between them is that the mini is a general purpose computer while the micro is generally made for a single purpose [control of traffic lights, elevators, microwave ovens, garage door openers, etc.].

Micros usually only include capabilities they actually need. Others are omitted because they are not needed and they cost money, but the basic ingredients of all computers are included [Input–Output, memory, control and arithmetic–logic unit]. The microcomputer often makes use of several microprocessor chips.

A microprocessor is a single chip, usually requiring some support chips to make a complete computer. Some of the newer microprocessors have all the necessary circuitry on one chip.

The circuitry of a microprocessor is accomplished by first making a master drawing 500 times as large as the actual chip. It is then reduced photographically to micro-miniature size and transferred to the chip by a technique similar to photo-engraving.

During actual manufacture, a single speck of dust can ruin a chip, so all work is done in "clean rooms" where the air is filtered and workers wear surgical type clothes.

Personal computers use microprocessors. Personal computers are generally single-user systems, so that the relatively low performance is not noticed. Sales of personal computers continue to grow as they are used widely in business, industry, schools and at home. It is interesting to note that the $3,000 [approximate figure] microprocessor-based personal computers of today are in many respects as powerful as the largest computers of fiteen or twenty years ago.

2

BASIC PROGRAM ELEMENTS

BASIC PROGRAM ELEMENTS

A. General

A programming language, like natural languages, is a tool for communication, not between people, but to enable humans to tell computers what work they want done and how it should be accomplished.

Learning a programming language is not unlike learning a natural language [such as Russian or Chinese]. First, the alphabet must be learned, then a basic vocabulary, followed by the fundamental rules for putting words together into meaningful statements.

A noticeable difference between programming languages and natural languages is that the rules for programming languages have few exceptions because they are generally the result of a careful design process, while natural languages evolve with the evolution of society. Learning a programming language is easier in many respects than learning a natural language. Programming language rules of syntax have few if any exceptions. Because of these strict rules, expressing a method of problem solution may be more difficult than a natural language solution.

B. Character Set

The alphabet recognized by the computer is called a character set. The basic character set recognized by the Ada language includes the 128 character ASCII character set. Not all 128 characters are used. The characters most commonly used consist of the following:

1.	Upper case letters	—the 26 letters of the alphabet. A through Z.
2.	Digits	—the 10 Arabic numerals, 0 through 9.
3.	Space character	—used as a separator between words, names and numbers.
4.	Special characters	—20 special characters:

```
        "  #  %  &  '  ( )  * +  ,  −  .  /  :  ;
        < =        >  _  |
```

The basic character set may be extended by adding the lower case letters of the alphabet and the following additional special characters:

```
        !  $  ?  @  [  \  ]  ⌃  '  {  }  ~
```

These characters are the graphic part of the standard ASCII character set. The complete ASCII character set may be found in Appendix B.

C. Identifiers

In this text, the extended character set will be used to emphasize the difference between language reserved words and programmer-chosen identifiers. Language reserved words [also called Key words] will be in lower case and programmer-chosen identifiers will be in upper case.

Reserved words are special words that may not be used as programmer devised names [identifiers]. These special words activate special compiler operations. A list of reserved words may be found in Appendix A.

Identifiers are arbitrary names used to name data units, loop parameters, constants, types, variables, labels, sub-programs, and program units in a program. In Ada, the character set is used to form identifiers according to the following rules:

1. An identifier may be of any length, but usually 31 or fewer characters are used.
2. The first character must be a letter.
3. After the first letter, other letters, digits, or the underscore may be used.
4. Most special characters may not be used. The few that may be used are best avoided.
5. Either upper or lower case letters may be used.
6. Identifiers must always be unique and different from all other identifiers in the program.
7. If an identifier is made up of two or more words, they are connected with underscores, but only one underscore between each word [as: TOTAL_AREA, INV_CTRL].
8. An underscore may not be followed by an underscore, nor may an identifier end with an underscore.

Choice of identifiers are important to good programming. If names are chosen well, they describe their role in the program. It is much easier to understand what a program is doing if the variables are called GROSS_INCOME, DEDUCTIONS, or NET_INCOME rather than if they were named X1, X2, X3. On the other hand, it is better not to use names which are too long and cumbersome.

Examples

Legal Identifiers

final_grade   target_direction_cosine   B770918
A2   ENGINE_TEMP   Circuit_Resistance   Average_Income

Illegal Identifiers

TIME@INT   _index   9P_RANGE   Pause__length   alpha_   2J
LAST_   FLAP;ANGLE

WORK AREA

Work these problems on scratch paper, then check your answers with the correct answers given on the following page.

1. Special words that are restricted from being used by the programmers as identifiers [names] are called _____.

2. Why may the following two identifiers not be used in the same program scope ?   set_up   SET_UP

3. Is there anything wrong with the following identifiers ? If so, what is wrong ?

   a. COsign   d. end_HOLD   g. X14_[2]
   b. K52?   e. 2TOTAL
   c. B52YX3   f. UPPER_LIMIT_OF_THE_RANGE

1. reserved words
2. they are identical — the compiler does not identify a difference between upper and lower case
3. a. OK
   b. should not use special characters
   c. OK, but not meaningful
   d. OK
   e. first position must be a letter
   f. OK, but getting too long
   g. special characters may not be used

D. Comments

An essential part of writing good programs is to include text not understood by the language. Such text sequences are called comments and are English language explanations specifying what the program [or a part of it] is doing.

Programming languages are designed to allow people to communicate with computers and often are not very good at communicating ideas between people. Ada is better than many at producing readable and understandable programs. A very important part of this ability is based on the use of comments by the programmer.

Comments are particularly helpful in reminding a programmer of various key steps in the program. They are of exceptional value if responsibility for a program moves from one person to another.

A comment statement begins with a double hyphen and ends with the end of a line.

Examples

```
- - This procedure computes the average of three input data items
- - and prints out the values obtained.
loop; - - loop through all elements
end loop; - - all elements processed
```

Comments have no effect on the program. They are inserted for information only and as a valuable form of internal documentation. A comment may appear anywhere in the program.

E. Numbers

The Ada language will accept two kinds of numbers:
Integers [whole numbers] — for exact computations
Real Numbers — for approximate computations

Specifics:
1. A real number is indicated in a program by the use of a decimal point.
2. Decimal numbers [base 10] may be used, or any other base numbers [2 through 16] may be used. If no base is indicated, decimal is the base that Ada will asume.

3. For bases above 10, the digits include the letters A through F, with the values of 10 through 15.

4. An exponent indicates the raising of a number by the power of 10. Only integer exponents are allowed.

5. The underscore character may be used occasionally for clarification purposes, but the underscore has no significance to the arithmetic or to the program.

Examples

263 1_000_000 56E2	Decimal integers [E is for exponent]
14.3E3 34.2 15.00	Decimal real numbers

Most of the time literal numbers of base 10 [decimal numbers] will be used. In more advanced applications, it may be necessary to use numeric literals of a base other than ten.

Based numbers are set off by a pair of pound signs (#), with the base written first in decimal. The base is always specified as a decimal number.

2#010101# 2#111101#	Binary based integer constants
8#46# 8#225#	Octal based integer constants
16#27F3# 16#4AEC#	Hexadecimal based integer constants
16#AE.BB#E2 [meaning: $AE.BB_{16} \times 16^2$]	Hex based real constant
2#1.110_101#E6 [$1.110\ 101_2 \times 2^6$]	Binary based real number

---

WORK AREA

Work these problems on scratch paper, then check your answers with the correct answers given on the following page.

1. A comment statement must always be preceded by _____ __.

2. Write the following in Ada acceptable form.

   a. 256   d. $4.AEB_{16} \times 16^2$

   b. 14.75×10^3 e. 275.5_8

   c. 1.001100_2 f. $111000_2 \times 2^4$

3. What kind of number is each of the above?

1.   double hyphen

2.   a.   256   d.   16#4.AEB#E2

     b.   14.75E3   e.   8#275.5#

     c.   2#1.001100#   f.   2#111000#E4

3.   a.   decimal integer   d.   hex real

     b.   decimal real   e.   octal real

     c.   binary real   f.   binary integer

F.   Delimiters

Delimiters are used, as needed, to separate parts of a program statement. Names, keywords and operators are separated in Ada by delimiters. An obvious delimiter is the space character which may occur between reserved words, identifiers and operators. Wherever one space is used, any number of spaces may be used. Comments also serve as spaces.

Delimiters consist of the following 16 special characters:

    & ' ( ) * + , - . / : ; < = > |

Delimiters also include the following 10 compound symbols

=>	arrow	:=	assignment
<< >>	label brackets	/=	not equal
< >	box	>=	greater than or equal
..	range indicator	<=	less than or equal
**	exponentiation		the space character

The meaning and use of the delimiters will be discussed in various sections to follow. They are used to terminate and separate identifiers, reserved words, phrases, expressions and statements in Ada.

G.   Numeric Literals

A literal is a group of digits or characters that have the same meaning logically as they do physically. For example, we may write the words "twenty five," but we usually write the literal 25. Numeric literals are used to give values to data units and in control statements to have something accomplished a certain number of times [10 times, for example].

In Ada, a literal is a piece of data that may not be changed by any operation in the program. A numeric literal may be either an integer or a real number. Conventional notation for decimal numbers is used, although commas are not allowed in large numbers. Instead, Ada allows the use of the underscore character [_] for clarity in large numbers.

Since representation of superscripts which denote exponents is difficult on most input and output devices, the character E is used to indicate that the numeric literal preceding the E is to be multiplied by 10 to the power following the E.

Generally, numeric literals are used to give initial values to variables or constants, or when comparison to a specific value is required. Also, when arithmetic operations with a certain value are needed.

Examples

Integer Literals:

17	255	6_845_279	0	12E5 [or 1_200_000]
1E3 [or 1000]		−163	−5E2 [or −500]	

Integer literals [by definition] may not have negative exponents, since this would make them rational numbers. However, negative exponents are allowed, as the following:

3E−5	[means 3/10_000]
22E−1	[means 22/10]

There is a great danger in using the above notation since these expressions may result in 0 [zero] if assigned to an integer type. It is better to use real literals for representing rational literals.

Real Literals:

17.0	255.0	471.028	0.0
32.78E12		1.07E−4	0.0237

WORK AREA

Work these problems on scratch paper, then check your answers with the correct answers given on the following page.

1. Write the following in a form permitted by Ada.
   a. 1,246,503
   b. 12**3

2. Change the following integer literals to real literals.
   a. 27
   b. 3_245
   c. 45E2

CORRECT ANSWERS

1. a. 1_246_503 or 1246503

  b. 12E3

2. a. 27.0   Note that the change is made
  b. 3_245.0   simply by adding a decimal point
  c. 45.0E2   in the appropriate position

H. Character Strings and Character Literals

If software systems were limited to numeric calculations alone, their range of application would be too limited. Characters and other non-numeric data are used in a great many applications.

Character literals are formed in Ada by using any one of the 95 ASCII characters [refer to Appendix B] including the space character, between single quotes.

Examples

'A' 'd' '1' '+' '$' ' ' '#'

If more than a single character is needed in a literal, several characters may be grouped into a character string. The string is enclosed by string bracket characters ("), which must be written at both the beginning and end of the string. Usually the double quote character is used as the string bracket character.

Examples

" " [empty string] "A" string of length 1

"special characters ! , & (} may appear in a string"

"A SHORT STRING"

"He said," "That's enough !" "

If a character string is longer than one line, the first line must be closed by the string bracket character, followed by the catenation* character (&). The catenation character is also used for including non-printable ASCII characters into character strings.

---

*The term catenate means to "link together," as in linking line one to line two. The & sign is used for this purpose.

Examples

"A VERY LONG STRING MAY BE BROKEN" &
"INTO SEVERAL PARTS" & "AND JOINED" &
"USING THE CATENATION CHARACTER"

ASCII.CR& "CONTROL CHARACTERS" & ASCII.BS &
"IN A STRING"

WORK AREA

Work these problems on scratch paper, then check your answers with the correct
answers given on the following page.

    1.   a. Character literals are enclosed between _____.

             b. Character strings are enclosed between _____.

    2. Write the following as character literals:

        a. P   d. $

        b. a   e. (

        c. 3   f. !

    3. Write the following as character strings:

        a. first class

        b. AB+/*—CD(4)

    4. What characters are used at the end of the first line if the character
        string is longer than a single line ?

27

1.   a.   two single quotes
        b.   two double quotes

2.   a.   'P'   d. '$'
        b.   'a'   e. '('
        c.   '3'   f. '!'

3.   a.   "first class"
        b.   "AB+/*−CD(4)"

4.   double quotes "followed by the catenation character & [called ampersand]. The ampersand does not have to be at the end of the first line; it may start the next line.

I.   Program Structure

     The basic program unit in Ada is the procedure. All Ada systems require at least one procedure although they may otherwise consist entirely of other types of program units. A single procedure, or the procedure which initiates other program units is called the main program.

     A procedure [like other program units] consists of two major parts, the declarative part [or interface] and the implementation part [body].

Example

A Simple Ada Procedure

     A semicolon is used to end all declarations and statements. The symbol := is the assignment delimiter (BIG is assigned the value 999). The colon separates a variable name (BIG) from a type name (BETA). Types and variables will be discussed in detail in Chapter 3.

```
declarative        procedure  MAIN  is
   part                type  BETA  is  NEW_INTEGER
[interface]
                       BIG : BETA ;
                       GROSS : BETA ;

implementation     begin
    part               BIG:=999;
  [body]               GROSS:=5000;
                           GROSS:=GROSS−BIG;
                   end  MAIN;
```

28

The example shows a simple Ada program illustrating the major parts of the Ada procedure. In the declarative part the data to be used is described, first as a type which denotes its characteristics and then as a variable or constant which provides their names. Many other things may also be declared. These will be discussed later in the text. The program unit's relationship to the rest of the system is defined in this part, hence the name interface.

The word begin starts the implementation part of the procedure. This is where the work accomplished by the procedure occurs. This part [known as the body of the procedure] sets forth a sequence of statements which describes the algorithm or process for accomplishing the work to be done.

Describing an algorithm in a programming language is called coding. To practiced software developers, coding is the easiest part of the job, but for beginners this can be a very difficult task until some experience is gained.

In subsequent chapters the student will be provided with the experience and skills to make coding a straightforward task. Additionally, it should provide a start toward the development of skills for solving the larger problems of software systems.

WORK   AREA

Work these problems on scratch paper, then check your answers with the correct answers given on the following page.

1. The executable part of a procedure is called ?

2. What is the purpose of the interface part of a procedure ?

3. In the example on the previous page:
    a. What type of number is represented by BETA ?
    b. What is the numeric value of GAMMA ?
    c. What is the name of the procedure ?
    d. Where do names such as BIG and GROSS come from ?
    e. What is the actual operation to be performed ?

1. implementation part or body

2. to describe the elements to be used in the body

3.   a.   integer
       b.   5000
       c.   MAIN
       d.   made up by the programmer
       e.   subtraction

Chapter 2 Summary

What has been discussed in this chapter are the atomic elements of Ada, the building blocks which are combined to form programs and software systems. The next level of structure is that of declarations and statements, which will be examined in detail in following chapters. Declarations and statements are combined to form program units and ultimately program units are combined to form the total software system.

The details of these basics are extremely important as they will be used continually throughout the problems and examples shown in the text. The student will become quite familiar with the contents of this chapter as he progresses through the following chapters.

Chapter 2 Quiz

Work these problems on scratch paper, then check your answers with the correct answers given on the following page.

1. Reserved words are also called Keywords. [true or false]
2. Reserved words are commonly used as identifiers. [true or false]
3. The space or blank is considered to be a character. [true or false]
4. Keywords activate compiler operations. [true or false]
5. The first position in an identifier must be a digit. [true or false]
6. Only upper case letters may be used in identifiers. [true or false]
7. Comments have no effect on the program. [true or false]
8. It is not really important to use comments. [true or false]
9. Delimiters are used to separate parts of program statements. [true or false]
10. A space is not considered to be a delimiter. [true or false]
11. A literal may not be changed by the program. [true or false]
12. Exponentiation is shown by the letter A. [true or false]
13. Character literals are placed between single quotes. [true or false]
14. Character strings are enclosed by single quotes. [true or false]
15. Indicate which of the following are real numbers:

    a.   126   c.   15E2

    b.   12.6   d.   1327E2

16. What is the base of the following numbers ?

    a.   8#327#   c.   5#024#

    b.   16#4A3#   d.   2#0100#

17. What are the two kinds of literals ?
18. What is the meaning of the term catenate ?
19. When is a character string to be used ?

CORRECT ANSWERS

1. true
2. false
3. true
4. true
5. false
6. false
7. true
8. false
9. true
10. false
11. true
12. false
13. true
14. false
15. b. and d. are real numbers
16. a. octal
    b. hexadecimal
    c. base 5
    d. binary
17. numeric and character
18. to link together
19. when the total string needs to be longer than one character

Any items that were missed should be reviewed by the student.

3

TYPES AND VARIABLES

TYPES AND VARIABLES

A. General

Programs consist of data and operations performed on the data. In this chapter the method of describing data will be shown. Once the data has been described, then the operations allowed on the data may be defined. These operations are combined in Ada statements to specify the algorithms which perform the desired data changes.

The internal representation of data in most computers is confined to only integer and floating point numbers. With these types of data computer hardware is very efficient. The myriad types of information that humans deal with are much, more complex comprising elements such as color, texture, names, addresses, natural language and so on.

The logical structure of human minds is better served by the use of many more types than integers or real numbers. The Ada language allows the programmer to describe and use many different types of data with the compiler translating these into the internal representation of the machine.

Program data has certain characteristics which represent the type of the data. Types aid the programmer in many ways. With each data type is associated a set of operations. For example, integers might have the following:

a.   arithmetic operations   (+, −, *, /, **)
b.   comparison operations   (=, > , < , /=, > =, < =)
c.   assignment operator   (:=)

A floating point type may have the same set of operations defined. While the symbols for the operations appear identical, this is more of a convenience to humans than a mathematical fact.

There is no problem as long as operations are performed on variables of the same type. Adding two integers and assigning the sum to a third causes no problem. Nor does subtracting two floating point numbers and assigning the difference to another floating point number. But what happens when a floating result is assigned to an integer variable [such as assigning 3.7 to an integer]? Integers have no fractional parts so what happens to the seven-tenths? Should it be dropped or rounded up to 4? In addition to this problem, what happens when the integer is converted back to floating point? Is it possible to get the seven-tenths back? Of course not.

Some applications might require these kinds of conversions. In some languages it is possible to introduce type conversions accidentally. This cannot happen in Ada; all type conversions must be done explicitly, and in a manner which is obvious to anyone who reads the program. This helps prevent many errors caused by implicit type conversions.

A type is simply a set of characteristics including the set of values a constant or variable may take. Types are used all the time; numbers may be natural, integer, rational, real or imaginary to name a few; a car may be a Buick, Datsun, Ford or Chevy; a human being may be male or female. Types help to distinguish classes of similar data.

In Ada, every piece of information has a type, which is given in a type declaration. A type declaration is made in the declarative part of an Ada program unit. Once a type declaration is made, then a variable or constant declaration may be made. This is also done in the declarative part of the program unit. The variable declaration must follow the type declaration that the variable will use.

Types may be predefined as programmer defined. Predefined types serve as the building blocks for programmer defined types. The predefined types include Boolean, integer, float, fixed and character. Each of the predefined types will be examined then the methods used to compose data descriptions will be shown.

Programmer defined types are derived from the predefined types, either by restricting the values of operations or by combining several types into a composite type. It is generally good programming practice for all types to be programmer defined, even if this is only restatement of the predefined qualities.

As the programmer gains experience, the advantages of restricting the allowable values and operations will become more obvious. By restricting the type to the smallest legal attributes, erroneous occurrences are more easily detected and handled with minimum disruption to the software system.

WORK AREA

1. Write the following predefined operators in arithmetic symbology:

    a. multiply   e. assignment
    b. exponent   f. divide
    c. greater than   g. less than or equal
    d. unequal   h. add

2. What is the purpose of type declarations?

3. Does a type declaration have to be specified for every piece of information to be used by the program?

4. A type declaration is made in what part of an Ada program?

5. What usually follows a type declaration?

6. Name some predefined types.

CORRECT ANSWERS

1. a. *   e. :=
    b. **   f. /
    c. >   g. <=
    d. /=   h. +

2. to specify the type to be used by the following variable or constant declaration

3. yes

4. declarative part

5. a variable declaration

6. Boolean, integer, floating point, fixed point, character

B. Boolean Type

Variables of the Boolean type may take only two values, true or false. False is arbitrarily defined to be less than true. Boolean variables are most often used to report the results of a test [such as: is X < Y? or does A = B?], or as flags [indicators that some event or condition has occurred].

The word Boolean comes from the name of an English clergyman and mathematician, George Boole, who lived in the early 19th century. In 1854, he published a book that was meant to be a mathematical analysis of logic. His book gathered dust until 1937, when Claude Shannon, a Bell Telephone Co. engineer, needed a method to simplify multiple switching circuits. He took Boole's original ideas and developed the logic now called Boolean logic [or Boolean algebra].

To declare a type using the Boolean predefined type is quite straightforward.

Examples

```
type FLAG is BOOLEAN ;
type SUPERVISOR_STATE is BOOLEAN ;
type OVER_LIMIT_FLAG is BOOLEAN ;
```

A variable of type FLAG may not be compared with a variable of type SUPERVISOR_STATE as each was declared to be a different predefined type. An explicit conversion would have to be accomplished to change the type of one so that both would be of the same type for comparison. Unlike the other predefined types, in practice the variable is often declared directly as Boolean.

Examples

Variables declared as predefined type Boolean:

```
CARRIER_LOST : BOOLEAN ;
MESSAGE_PENDING : BOOLEAN ;
SORT_COMPLETE : BOOLEAN ;
```

36

An intial value may be given when declaring a variable. To initialize a variable, a value is assigned to it at the time it is declared.

Examples

SYSTEM_ARMED : BOOLEAN := FALSE ;
FOUND : BOOLEAN := FALSE
QUEUE_EMPTY : BOOLEAN := TRUE ;

The operations defined for BOOLEAN types are assignment, comparison and logical operations AND, OR and XOR.

WORK AREA

1. Name the Boolean values.

2. Declare a Boolean type called:
    a. CHECK
    b. SUM

3. Declare a Boolean variable called:
    a. SEQUENCE
    b. HOLD_OUT

4. Initialize SEQUENCE to false and HOLD_OUT to true.

1. true — false

2. a. type CHECK is BOOLEAN ;
   b. type SUM is BOOLEAN ;

3. a. SEQUENCE : BOOLEAN ;
   b. HOLD_OUT : BOOLEAN ;

4. a. SEQUENCE : BOOLEAN := FALSE
   b. HOLD_OUT : BOOLEAN := TRUE

C. Integer Type

The predefined integer type includes the values of all the positive and negative integers for the computer being used. Integer types are used to count items or occurrences, or to indicate rank or order in the same manner that integers are used in areas other than programming.

Integer Declaration Format

type T is range L . . H ;

Explanation:

type	— keyword indicating type declaration
T	— the type name invented by the programmer
is	— keyword connecting to the next item
range	— keyword indicating the actual range to follow
L	— lowest value
H	— highest value [L must not be greater than H]

Type T will include all values from L through H inclusive.

Example
type BASEBALL_INNING is range 1 . . 9 ;

A variable of type BASEBALL_INNING may take only the values 1,2,3,4,5,6,7,8,9. Trying to give a variable of this type a value of 10 would result in an error (NUMERIC_ERROR).

Examples

type INTERRUPT_LEVEL is range 0 . . 255 ;
type SMALL_INTEGER is range −256 . . 256 ;
— — there are 513 possible values in SMALL_INTEGER
— — [don't forget zero]
type DAY_OF_YEAR is range 1 . . 366 ;
type DAY_OF_MONTH is range 1 . . 31 ;
— — although these both may refer to the same day,
— — they are not the same type

1. Subtype

Sometimes the programmer may need only part of the values of a type. The subtype allows a part of the range of a declared type to be used. Choosing a subset of the values of a declared type to make a subtype is said to be constraining that type.

Because they are the same type, subtypes may be compared and assigned to each other, as long as the constraints of both subtypes are satisfied.

Format

Subtype T1 is T range L . . R ;

Explanation:

subtype	– keyword indicating subtype name to follow
T1	– subtype name
is	– keyword connector
T	– type name
range	– keyword indicating the range to follow
L . . R	– lowest to highest range

Examples

Subtype DAY_OF_NORMAL_YEAR is DAY_OF_YEAR range 1 . . 365 ;
Subtype DAY_OF_FEBRUARY is DAY_OF_MONTH range 1 . . 28 ;
Subtype DAY_OF_SEPTEMBER is DAY_OF_MONTH range 1 . . 30 ;
Subtype SIMPLE_INTEGERS is SMALL_INTEGER range − 10 . . 10 ;
Subtype SMALL_NATURAL is SMALL_INTEGER range 1 . . 256 ;
Subtype SIMPLE_NATURAL is SMALL_NATURAL range 1 . . 10 ;

Declaring a variable of type integer or of a declared type is similar to declaring a Boolean variable. Because a wider range of values is available, the programmer may choose to constrain a variable to a set of values without declaring a type or subtype. Like the Boolean variable, the integer variable may be given an initial value.

To declare a variable of either predefined type or user defined type, the variable is written before the type name and the two are separated by a colon.

General Format

variable_name : type_name := initial_value

The initial value is optional. It permits a programmer to give a value to the variable at the time it is declared [before it is used]. It is a good policy to give all variables initial values.

Constants are declared with the same form as variables except that an initial value is required and the reserved word constant must be used before the type name.

General Format

constant_value : constant type_name := initial_value

Examples

1. Constant Declarations:

STRETCH_INNING : constant BASEBALL_INNING := 7 ;
− − constant declaration of user defined type
ONE, UN, EINS, UNO : constant := 1 ;
− − constant declaration of type integer. Four constants are
− − declared, each having the value 1.
SECOND : constant DAY_OF_MONTH := 2 ;
− − constant declaration of a subtype

2. Variable Declarations:

BIG_INNING : BASEBALL_INNING ;

CHAPTER_NUMBER : SMALL_INTEGER range 1 . . 25 ;
− − a constrained variable declaration using a declared type

LABOR_DAY ; DAY_OF_SEPTEMBER ;
− − variable declaration

DISK_ACCESS : SMALL_NATURAL ;
− − variable declaration

WORK AREA

Problem Statement:

A program is to be written to do class schedules. Each student may take a minimum of one course and a maximum of six courses. There are a minimum of twenty courses offered and a maximum of 125 courses. Each class may have up to thirty students, but must have a minimum of five. However, art classes may have a maximum of twenty and music classes may have a maximum of ten students.

1. Create integer types [or subtypes] for:
   a. the number of courses a particular student has been assigned.
   b. the number of courses offered.
   c. the number of students in a class.
   d. the number of students in a music or art class.

2. Create appropriate variables for the number of students in:
   a. a Civil War History class
   b. a basic drawing class
   c. the number of classes Jedediah Daniels is taking
   d. a Calculus I class
   e. a Music Theory I class

It is unlikely that the names chosen by any student would match that of the authors or fellow students, but they should convey similar information.

CORRECT ANSWERS

1. a. type NUM_STUDENT_COURSES_ASSIGNED is range 1 .. 6 ;
  b. type NUM_COURSES_OFFERED is range 20 .. 125 ;
  c. type NUM_STUDENTS_IN_CLASS is range 5 .. 30 ;
  d. subtype NUM_ART_STUDENTS is NUM_STUDENTS_IN_CLASS
     range 5 .. 20 ;
    subtype NUM_MUSIC_STUDENTS is NUM_STUDENTS_IN_CLASS
     range 5 .. 10 ;

2. a. NUM_CIVIL_WAR_HISTORY_STUDENTS : NUM_STUDENTS_IN_CLASS ;
  b. NUM_BASIC_DRAWING_STUDENTS : NUM_ART_STUDENTS ;
  c. NUM_J_DANIELS_CLASSES : NUM_STUDENT_COURSES_ASSIGNED ;
  d. NUM_CALCULUS_I_STUDENTS : NUM_STUDENTS_IN_CLASS ;
  e. NUM_MUSIC_THEORY_I_STUDENTS : NUM_MUSIC_STUDENTS ;

D. Floating Point Type

Integer types are used for counting applications where the items being counted are discrete objects or events. Many applications require measurements which are not simple tallies. For approximate measurements real numbers are used.

In Ada, floating point numbers answer this requirement. Floating point is so named because the decimal point moves [or floats] so that the most significant digits in the number are preserved.

Floating point types are declared by describing a model number. The model number describes how many decimal digits of accuracy will be maintained through all operations on variables of this type. The model number also describes the scale of the number using the keyword-range. The scale describes the values the numbers may take.

For example, a real number may have five digits of accuracy, but those five digits may be any one of many combinations:

Examples

				rewritten using exponent	
from:	0.0	to:	10,000	from: 0.0	to: 1.0000E5
	2.0000		3.0000	2.0000	3.0000EO
	292,000.0		392,000.0	2.9200E6	3.9200E6
	.00010000		.00099999	1.0000E−4	9.9999E−4

These numbers may be scaled by using the E [exponent] indicator and allowing the decimal point to float. See the rewritten examples above.

The exponent may be thought of as a scaling factor since it describes the approximate size of the number. However, a scaling factor may be more complicated than just an exponent.

Unlike the integer, the number of possible values of the floating point type is not being specified. What is being specified is the magnitude and accuracy of numbers of the type.

42

The model number is in a sense a contract that the numbers in a certain range will always be at least as accurate as the digits specify. There may be millions of possible values between the endpoints of a range, but each number will have the accuracy of the type.

The required accuracy is specified by the use of the keyword-digits.

Examples

type REAL is digits 8 ;
- - this is a floating point number with only the accuracy specified

type VELOCITY is REAL digits 5 range -1.0E3 . . 1.0E10 ;
- - Here is a floating point type created by constraining another floating
- - point type in accuracy and scale

type ANGLE is digits 5 range -360.0 . . 360.0 ;
- - This specifies both the required accuracy and the range of values

type VOLUME is digits 3 range 0.0 . . 1.00E4 ;
- - Values above 999 will have only the three left digits
- - guaranteed accurate. The fourth digit may or may not be accurate.

WORK AREA

1. In addition to the name, what is usually specified for a floating point type ?

2. Write a floating point type declaration named HOLD with a range from zero through 4.2 to the second power.

3. Add an accuracy constraint of 2 to the above type declaration

CORRECT ANSWERS

1. accuracy and magnitude of the numbers

2. type HOLD range 0.0 . . 4.2E2 ;
   — this being floating point, even the zero must be
   — written with a decimal point

3. type HOLD is digits 2 range 0.0 . . 4.2E2 ;

---

1. Variable Declarations

Just as with integers, variables are declared using the types that were previously declared. They may be further constrained and subtypes may be used as needed.

Examples

COEFFICIENT : REAL range 0.0 . . 1E7 ;
— variable of type REAL with range constraint

subtype SHORT_REAL is REAL digits 3 ;
— subtype with constrained accuracy

AIRSPEED : VELOCITY range 0.0 . . 1500.0 ;
— variable with scale constraint

subtype LEFT is ANGLE range 90.0 . . 180.0 ;

Real types are often called approximate numbers since they are used to quantify data whose measurement becomes uncertain after some specified accuracy. Floating point is used when numbers vary greatly in scale but they must be operated on together.

Both integers and floating point numbers may be operated on by the basic arithmetic functions +, −, *, / .

1. Write the subtype declarations for type ANGLE using the following information

    ACUTE has a scale constraint of 0.0 to 90.0

    RIGHT has a scale constraint of 90.0 to 90.0

    OBTUSE has a scale constraint of 90.0 to 180.0

2. Write a variable declaration called SUMMARY of type REAL with an accuracy constraint of 2 and a range constraint from 0.0 to 1 to the 5th power.

3. A tracking system is written which must serve on land, sea and air. It is known that:

    [a] ships may go 15 knots backwards and 100 knots forward,

    [b] submarines may go 10 knots backwards and 80 knots forward,

    [c] land vehicles may go 50 knots backwards and 125 knots forward,

    [d] aircraft may travel 30 knots backwards and 2000 knots forward,

    [e] satellites may travel at 25,000 knots.

    Respond to the following statements:

    a. Declare a single type and then write constrained variable declarations for each vehicle.

    b. Declare a single type and appropriate subtypes for each vehicle.

    c. Declare separate types for each vehicle.

CORRECT ANSWERS

1.   Subtype ACUTE is ANGLE range 0.0 . . 90.0 ;
   Subtype RIGHT is ANGLE range 90.0 . . 90.0 ;
   Subtype OBTUSE is ANGLE range 90.0 . . 180.0 ;

2.   SUMMARY : REAL is digits 2 range 0.0 . . 1E5 ;

3. a.   type VEHICLE_SPEED is digits 9 range −150 . . 25_000 ;
   SHIP_SPEED : VEHICLE_SPEED range −15 . . 100 ;
   SUB_SPEED : VEHICLE_SPEED range −10 . . 80 ;
   LAND_SPEED : VEHICLE_SPEED range −50 . . 125 ;
   AIRCRAFT_SPEED : VEHICLE_SPEED range −30 . . 2_000 ;
   SATELLITE_SPEED : VEHICLE_SPEED range 0 . . 25_000 ;

    b.   type VEHICLE_SPEED is digits 9 range −150 . . 25_000 ;
   subtype SEA_SPEED : VEHICLE_SPEED range −15 . . 100 ;
   subtype LAND_SPEED : VEHICLE_SPEED range −50 . . 125 ;
   subtype AIR_SPEED : VEHICLE_SPEED range −30 . . 25_000 ;

    c.   type SHIP_SPEED is digits 9 range −15 . . 100 ;
   type SUB_SPEED is digits 9 range −10 . . 80 ;
   type LAND_SPEED is digits 9 range   −50 . . 125 ;
   type AIRCRAFT_SPEED is digits 9 range −30 . . 2_000 ;
   type SATELLITE_SPEED is digits 9 range 0 . . 25_000 ;

E. Fixed Point Type

Fixed point numbers also have fractional parts. In some applications numbers have fractional parts, but there is a known accuracy of the fraction. In such cases, the decimal point may be thought of as being fixed and these numbers are said to be fixed point numbers.

As an example, in a bank account the money is measured in dollars and cents. It is meaningful to speak of an account with $132.77, but not $132.770026.

The normally accepted minimum increment when reporting a bank account is one cent or .01 dollar. Thus if two bank accounts have different amounts of money then the minimum difference, or delta [as it is known in engineering] is .01. Since the fractional increment is known, calculations will result in numbers which are accurate to .01, each having two decimal places of accuracy.

In Ada, fixed point numbers are declared by specifying the delta [or minimum difference] in the fractional part of the range, which describes the scale of numbers.

Fixed point numbers behave much like integers, although they look like real numbers. Specifying the delta and the range actually describes the set of values the type may take.

Examples

1. type DOLLARS is delta .01 range 0.0 . . 1_000_000 ;
2. type VOLT is delta .125 range 0 . . 10_000 ;
3. type ALTITUDE is delta .01 range 0 . . 10_000 ;
4. type MESSAGE_UNIT is delta .1 range 0 . . 1_000 ;

If an attempt is made to assign a value having more fractional numbers than the number declared, the excess low-order [least significant] numbers will be truncated and lost.

WORK AREA

1. What differentiates fixed point numbers from floating point numbers ?

2. What is the meaning of the term delta ?

3. type SMALL_ACCOUNT is delta .05 range 0 . . 10.00 ;
   How many values of a variable of type SMALL_ACCOUNT are there ?

4. type WEIGHT is delta .3 range −9 . . 19 ;
   How many values may a variable of type WEIGHT take ?

CORRECT ANSWERS

1. The accuracy of the fractional part is known in fixed point

2. The minimum difference.

3. 201 [0.00, 0.05, 0.10, ... 1.00, 1.05, 1,10, ... 9.55, 10.00]

4. 94

F. Enumeration Types

In Ada, the <u>enumeration</u> type allows the collection and use of logically related names as the values of a data type. It is called enumeration type because each value the type can have must be listed [or enumerated] in the type definition.

There are two predefined enumeration types: Boolean and Character. The Boolean type has been discussed earlier in this Chapter. The Character type can use both identifiers and character literals as values.

In examining sets of characters and numbers it can be seen that there is usually an order relationship existing [1 < 2, 2 < 3, etc. or A comes before B, B comes before C, etc.] Some of the data types have a fixed number of values: the set of characters includes A–Z, a–z, 1–10 and special characters, a total of 128. A character can be nothing else but one of these.

There are other groups of things which are logically related and have a fixed number of values. For example, the colors of a rainbow, the brand names of cars produced by General Motors, or the names of positions on a football team.

It is easier to think of Chevrolet, Pontiac, Oldsmobile, Cadillac, or tackle, guard, center than to see that the value of CAR_MAKE is 3 and then associate it with a name. This may cause confusion in a long program because the programmer may not remember whether 3 means Pontiac or Oldsmobile.

General Format

type ENUMERATION_TYPE_NAME is [list of values] ;

The order in which the values are written is important, as this forms the basis for the order relation of the set of values. The lowest value is written first and value increases from left to right.

Examples

type GM_CARS is (CHEVROLET, PONTIAC, OLDSMOBILE, CADILLAC) ;
type FOOTBALL_POSITIONS is (END, TACKLE, GUARD, CENTER,
    FLANKER, HALFBACK, FULLBACK, QUARTERBACK) ;
type TREE is (REDWOOD, PINE, OAK) ;

The order relationship holds true only for values [and variables] of the same type. Comparing PINE to OLDSMOBILE makes no sense and would cause an error due to mismatched types.

Two enumeration types may use the same value, but each one must be fully qualified so that it may be distinguished from the other.

Example

Suppose there is a type declared as follows:

type BASKETBALL_POSITIONS is (GUARD, CENTER, FORWARD) ;

The values GUARD and CENTER overload the same values in FOOTBALL_POSITIONS. When using the values which are overloaded, the fully qualified name must be used.

```
F : FOOTBALL_POSITIONS ;
B : BASKETBALL_POSITIONS ;

    F . CENTER /= B .CENTER
    F . GUARD /= B . GUARD
```

WORK AREA

1. What are the two predefined enumeration types ?

2. What is the difference between the two types ?

3. If range is specified, how must the range limits be ordered ?

4. A program is to be written to control traffic at an intersection using traffic lights. The traffic lights may have the values red, yellow, green and left turn.

Write an enumeration type declaration for the traffic light.

CORRECT ANSWERS

1. Boolean and character

2. Boolean uses true-false only
   Character type uses any character in the alphabet, any number or any special character, in any combination

3. lowest to highest

4. type TRAFFIC_LIGHT is (RED, YELLOW, GREEN, LEFT_TURN) ;

Enumeration variables may be defined in the same manner as declaring an enumeration type, by using a value list.

Examples

USED_CAR : GM_CARS ;
PRESTIGE_CAR : constant GM_CARS := CADILLAC ;

OFFENSIVE_TEAM : FOOTBALL_POSITIONS ;
BACKFIELD : FOOTBALL_POSITIONS range FLANKER . . QUARTERBACK ;
    -- BACKFIELD may take values FLANKER, HALFBACK, FULLBACK
    -- and QUARTERBACK

CONIFER : TREE range REDWOOD . . PINE ;

In specifying a range constraint, the range limits must be given in the proper order: lowest value to highest value.

Variables may be made enumeration variables by specifying their values.

Examples

RELEASE : (TRUE, FALSE) ;
SWITCH : (OFF, ON) ;
DEVICE_STATUS : (OFF, IDLE, BUSY, WAIT) ;
PAPER : (WHITE, LINED, COLORED) ;

WORK AREA

1. Well known dog breeds include:

    terrier, shepherd, collie, doberman, bulldog, blood hound,

    retriever, pointer and poodle

    a. Write an enumeration type declaration called DOG_BREED
        which can take these values.

    b. Declare a variable called HUNTING_DOG which includes
        BLOODHOUND, RETRIEVER and POINTER.

2. Write a type called LANGUAGE_NAME which can take the values:
    BASIC, FORTRAN, APT, PLI, JOVIAL, CMS2, ADA, C

3. Write a variable declaration for a variable called DOD_LANGUAGE
    which can have the values ADA, JOVIAL and CMS2, using the
    type declaration of problem 2 above.

4. type SCREEN_COLOR is (BLACK, WHITE, RED, GREEN, BLUE) ;
    MONOCHROME : SCREEN_COLOR range BLACK . . WHITE ;
    COLOR : SCREEN_COLOR ;

    a. What values may MONOCHROME take ?

    b. What values may COLOR take ?

    c. FLAG : SCREEN_COLOR range WHITE . . GREEN ;
        What values can FLAG take that MONOCHROME
        can also take ?

CORRECT ANSWERS

1.   a.   type DOG_BREED is (TERRIER, SHEPHERD, COLLIE,
                 DOBERMAN, BULLDOG, BLOODHOUND, RETRIEVER,
                 POINTER, POODLE) ;

      b.   HUNTING_DOG : DOGBREED range BLOODHOUND . .
                 POINTER) ;

2.   type LANGUAGE_NAME is (BASIC, FORTRAN, APT, PLI,
            JOVIAL, CMS2, ADA, C) ;

3.   DOD_LANGUAGE : LANGUAGE_NAME range JOVIAL . .
            ADA;

4.   a. BLACK, WHITE
      b. BLACK, WHITE, RED, GREEN, BLUE
      c. WHITE

Chapter 3 Summary

The method of describing the various types of data is covered in this chapter with the exception of composite types, which will be covered in Chapter 4. Type definitions are integral parts of every Ada program, making the study of this Chapter extremely important.

CHAPTER 3 QUIZ

1. Give the general type of variable which would be most suited to the following situations:

    a.   The variable is used to count the items being read from a list.

    b.   The variable represents the state of a switch; open or closed.

    c.   The variable represents devices to be communicated with: terminal, printer, disk drive, tape drive, card reader.

    d.   The variable is used to calculate very large values of an approximate nature.

    e.   The variable is used to hold the value of measurements made by a device which has a resolution of .0007 between measurements.

2. type CLOUD is digits 5 ;

    a. Could range 1E7 . . 1E10 be legally added to the declaration?

    b. GRAY : CLOUD ; -- CLOUD is without the range in "a"
       above
       GRAY := 8274901 ;

       What value would be stored in GRAY?

    c. CUMULUS, NIMBUS : CLOUD ;
       CUMULUS := 24.3879E-2 ;
       NIMBUS := 73.2678E5 ;
       NIMBUS := NIMBUS + CUMULUS ;

       What value is in NIMBUS?

3. Write the equivalent decimal value, given the exponent:

    a. 62.984E1   e. 62.984E2   i. 62.984E7

    b. 62.984E0   f. 62.984E3   j. 62.984E9

    c. 62.984E-1   g. 62.984E4   k. 62.984E-5

    d. 62.984E-2   h. 62.984E5

4. Type SIGNAL_LEVEL is delta .025 range 5 . . 12 ;
    How many values may a variable of type SIGNAL_LEVEL take?

5. type ACCESS_RIGHTS is (PUBLIC, READ_ONLY, WRITE_ONLY,
                        DELETE, READ_WRITE_DELETE) ;

    a. Defining a constant:
       LOWEST_ACCESS_RIGHT : constant ACCESS_RIGHT :=_____ ;
       What value should be used ?

    b. Defining another constant:
       HIGHEST_ACCESS_RIGHT : constant ACCESS_RIGHT := _____ ;
       What value should be used ?

CORRECT ANSWERS

1.   a.   Integer
       b.   Boolean
       c.   Enumeration type
       d.   Floating point
       e.   Fixed point

2.   a.   yes
       b.   82749E2
       c.   73267E6

3.

a.	629.84	e.	62.984	i.	.00062984
b.	6298.4	f.	6.2984	j.	.0000062984
c.	62984.	g.	.62984	k.	629840000.
d.	629840.	h.	.062984		

4.   280 values

5.   a.   PUBLIC
       b.   READ_WRITE_DELETE

4

STATEMENTS, STRINGS, AND COMPOSITE TYPES

STATEMENTS, STRINGS AND COMPOSITE TYPES

A. Statements

Types and variables describe the forms that data may take. The transformations and changes that occur in the program are not caused by types and variables, but are the result of the program statements. Statements are the instructions used to change data or to control the order of execution of the statements.

Statements are composed of expressions which are joined by operators. The operator which changes the value of a variable is assignment [:=]. Assignment causes the variable on the left of the operator symbol [:=] to take the value of the expression on the right. The expression to the right remains unchanged.

The statement X := Y ; is read "X takes the value of Y" [or X gets Y]. The value of the variable on the left of the assignment operator is replaced with a new value while the old value is destroyed. The source of the new value is not changed in the process. This is the rule of destructive read in, non-destructive read out.

As an example, consider the statement X := Y ; and assume that X = 43 and Y = 51 before the statement is executed. After execution of the statement, X will contain the value 51 and Y will contain the value 51. The 43 originally in X will have disappeared.

This type of assignment statement is quite useful for transferring values from one variable to another, but often it is necessary to modify the value of a variable or combine it in some way before giving the value to the variable to the left of the operator [called the target variable]. More complex assignment statements are formed using the arithmetic operators that were discussed briefly in Chapter 2.

+ [add]   − [subtract]   * [multiply]   / [divide]   ** [exponent]

Ada expressions must adhere to the following rules:
[1]   no characters may be physically above or below the line. The statement may require several text lines.
[2]   every operation must be identified using the appropriate operator [implied operations are not allowed, such as 2X meaning 2 * X]
[3]   the original order of the operations should be observed.

Arithmetic operations in Ada [as in mathematics] have a well defined rank of execution, called operator precedence.   Below is the precedence in Ada:

Operators	Operation	Rank
**	exponentiation	first
*	multiplication	2
/	division	2
+ , −	unary plus and minus signs	3
+	addition	last
−	subtraction	last

56

Writing mathematical expressions requires a little interpretation, but is generally a straightforward process. Figuring out the mathematics is usually the hard part.

Example

$$\frac{8 \ X^{15}}{a + b}$$

Step-by-step interpretation: The 15 is a superscript indicating exponentiation – use ** ; 8 X means 8 times X – use * operator; a + b is below a divide line – use / operator. Thus far, the following is shown: 8 * X ** 15 / a + b. If this were executed as it is now written, the original order of operations would not be observed because everything before the divide operator would be divided by a and then b would be added, resulting in an incorrect interpretation and an incorrect result.

Changing the precedence is done by using parentheses. The term or terms in parentheses are always evaluated first, therefore they are used to force the a + b to be interpreted together as shown here:

$$8 * X ** 15 / (a + b)$$

If there is a parenthesized term inside another set of parentheses, evaluation begins with the innermost and proceeds outward.

Example

$$(X + 6 * (Y - 3) / 4 * Y) * (Y + 6) / Y$$

The order of evaluation would be:

Y - 3, that result multiplied by 6, that result divided by 4 * Y and then added to X. This completes the left portion of the evaluation. Next Y is added to 6, then divided by Y. This result is multiplied by the previous result.

If X = 2 and Y = 4, the result would be:

$4 - 3 = 1$	$Y - 3$
$6 * 1 = 6$	$6 (Y - 3)$
$4 * 4 = 16$	$4 * Y$
$6 / 16 = 3/8$	$6 (Y - 3) / 4Y$
$2 + 3/8 = 2\,3/8$	$X + 6 (Y - 3) / 4Y$
$4 + 6 = 10$	$Y + 6$
$10 / 4 = 5/2$	$Y + 6 / Y$
$2\,\frac{3}{8} * \frac{5}{2} = \frac{95}{16}$	$(X + 6 (Y - 3) / 4Y) * (Y + 6) / Y$

The main task of the parentheses is to provide the capability of modifying the order of precedence of operations. In very complex expressions, parentheses should be used for clarity, to clearly indicate to the human programmer which operations are to be performed, in what sequence, on the variables.

Parentheses cost no operating time during execution of the program and their use often allows the correct expression to be written quickly and accurately. When in doubt, parenthesize. Care must be taken to match parends in each statement. Every left parend must have a matching right parend in the same statement.

Examples

$Y = X^4 + 4$ would be written $\qquad$ Y := X ** 4 + 4 ;

$Z = (X^2 - 1)(Y^2 + 3)$ would be written $\qquad$ Z := (X ** 2 − 1) * (Y ** 2 + 3) ;

WORK AREA

1. Write the following as Ada assignment statements

    a. $S = \dfrac{P^3 r}{S^2}$

    b. $E = \dfrac{\left[1 - \frac{1}{n}\right]^2}{\left[1 + \frac{1}{n}\right]^2}$

    c. $X = \dfrac{1}{1 + \dfrac{1}{2 + t}}$

2. Write an assignment statement which calculates the shaded area below and puts the value into the variable SHADED_AREA. Write a type declaration and variable declarations which are compatible.

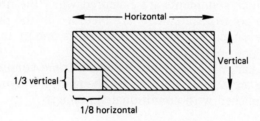

59

CORRECT ANSWERS

1.   a.   S := P ** 3 * r / S ** 2 ;

       b.   E := [1 − 1 / n] ** 2 / [1 + 1 / n] ** 2 ;

       c.   X := 1 / [1 + 1 / [2 + t]] ;

2.   type DIMENSIONS is REAL range 0 . . 10_000 ;

      HORIZ, VERT, SHADED_AREA : DIMENSIONS ;

      SHADED_AREA := HORIZ * VERT − [VERT / 3] * [HORIZ / 8] ;

---

1. Control Statements

If twenty-five assignment statements [or two or fifty] were written consecutively, they would be executed in the order that they appear on the page from top to bottom. The order of statements as they are written on paper is called the static order of the program.
      The order in which statements are executed when the program is run is called the dynamic order. If no control statements are included in the program, the static and dynamic order will be the same. Sequential execution is one of the basic control structures of a program.
      The ability to change the sequence based on some condition is a powerful programming tool. There are several methods of changing the dynamic order of execution. Changes are accomplished with conditional statements.

Basic Format

if CONDITION_EXPRESSION then CONDITIONAL_ACTION ;
end if ;

Explanation:

      if − then − required keywords
      For every if there must be an end if.
      The CONDITION_EXPRESSION evaluates to a Boolean value of True or False. When the value is True, the CONDITIONAL_ACTION will be accomplished. Otherwise the next statement to be executed would be the one following the end if statement.

Example

FINISHED , DONE ; Boolean ;

.

.

.

if FINISHED then DONE := TRUE ;
end if ;

.

.

if DONE then QUIT ;
end if;

Although this statement is useful it is limited in scope. Also, to be complete, each if must have an end if.

Setting Boolean values to true or false covers a limited range of possible conditions. Often it is necessary to make a choice based on the relationship of two or more values.

As an example, consider a program that is controlling the flight of an airplane. Periodically, a value must be obtained for the present altitude and this must be compared to the altitude value listed in the flight plan. If the present altitude is less than the planned altitude then the aircraft must climb. Otherwise, if the craft is at or above the planned altitude, it is safe from colliding with a mountain so no action is taken.

To write this kind of relationship, operators are needed which allow for the comparison of values. Relational operators are used to make these types of comparisons. They were mentioned briefly in Chapter 2 and are repeated here.

>	greater than	>=	greater than or equal
<	less than	<=	less than or equal
=	equal	/=	not equal

Using relational operators, comparison may be made between two variables, a variable and a constant, a variable and an expression, two expressions, etc., etc. The relational operator tests the proposed relationship and replaces it with a value of true if it succeeds, or false if it fails.

WORK AREA

1. What are the keywords used for a basic conditional statement ?

2. If STAT then JUMP ;
    end if ;
    COMP : . . . . .

    a. if STAT   is true what will happen ?
    b. if STAT   is false what will happen ?

61

CORRECT ANSWERS

1.   if then end if

2.   a.   the program will go to JUMP

      b.   the program will go to COMP

Example

Using a relational operator

if A   B then TRUE_BRANCH ;
Z := - - - - -
-- A and B must be of the same type [defined previously]
-- Suppose A = 5 and B = 7, then A   B would be true and the
-- statements following <u>then</u> would be executed.
-- However, if A = 7 and B = 5, then A   B would be false
-- and execution would continue with the statement Z := . . .

Some legal comparisons are:

    if A   7000 then - - -
    if A   B + 932 then - - -
    if A   = B + C then - - -
    if A   = 3 * [B + C — 17] then - - -
    if A + B   = C ** 2 then - - -
    if A + B /= [C + D] / 12 then - - -
    if A / B   C * D + 41 then - - -

Arithmetic operators have higher precedence than relational operators; the arithmetic is accomplished before the comparison. Precedence can be changed by the use of parentheses. In later pages, the method of combining several comparisons using logical operators with Boolean values will be shown.

Returning to the altitude control problem on the previous page, now it is possible to express the comparison that needs to be made. If the flight plan calls for flight at 5000 meters, the following Ada statements can be used:

62

```
type ALTITUDE_TYPE is INTEGER range 0 . . 50_000 ;
CURRENT_ALTITUDE, PLANNED_ALTITUDE : ALTITUDE_TYPE ;
     .
     .
     .

PLANNED_ALTITUDE := 5000 ; --THE ALTITUDE FROM THE FLIGHT PLAN
     .
     .
     .

if CURRENT_ALTITUDE < PLANNED_ALTITUDE then CLIMB ;
end if ;
--next statements in the program
     .
     .
```

     If the current altitude is 3000 meters, the test would succeed and the CLIMB statement would be executed. However, if the current altitude is 6000 meters, then the CLIMB statement would be skipped and execution would continue with the statements after the comment "NEXT STATEMENTS IN THE PROGRAM".
     This is not a realistic solution to the flight control problem because the program would cause the aircraft to climb or do nothing. In a climb it would never level off. The comparison must be extended to other possibilities including when the aircraft is at the desired altitude or above it. The flight plan problem will be continued on the next page.

WORK AREA

1. Using the following relational statement and values of A = 2, B = 3, C = 4, D = 1 :

   if A + B > C * D then MOVE ;
   end if;

   a.   Where will the program go ?
   b.   Changing the operator to < , where will the program go ?
   c.   Changing the operator to > =, where will the program go ?
   d.   Changing the operator to /=, where will the program go ?

2. Which operators have higher precedence, relational or arithmetic ?

3. D := 0 ;

   [1]   if A * B > C then D := 1 ;
   [2]   if A * C > B then D := 2 ;
   [3]   if B * C > A then D := 3 ;

   Given the values of A, B, C, what value of D will be obtained ?

   a.   A = 3, B = 4, C = 15
   b.   A = 3, B = 12, C = 01

CORRECT ANSWERS

1.   a.   to MOVE
      b.   to next statement in sequence
      c.   to MOVE
      d.   to MOVE

2. arithmetic

3.   a.   [1] 0   b. [1] 1
            [2] 2   [2] 0
            [3] 3   [3] 0

---

a. ELSE clause

Another clause may be added to the if statement called the else clause. This allows a two way choice to be made based on the value of the condition. If the condition is true, the action after the "then" is accomplished. If the condition tested is false, the statements after the "else" are performed.

General Format

```
if   <condition>   then   <statements performed when true>   ;
else   <statements performed when false>   ;
end if ;
```

In the altitude problem, if it is decided to level off at the current altitude or above it, the decision can be expressed as follows:

```
type ALTITUDE_TYPE is INTEGER range 0 . . 50_000 ;
CURRENT_ALTITUDE, PLANNED_ALTITUDE : ALTITUDE_TYPE ;
        .
        .
        .
PLANNED_ALTITUDE := 5000 ;
        .
        .
        .
if CURRENT_ALTITUDE  <  PLANNED_ALTITUDE then CLIMB ;
else LEVEL_OFF ;
end if ;
--NEXT STATEMENTS
```

In this case if the current altitude was 3000 meters, the craft would climb. If at 5000 meters, it would level off, or if at 7500 meters, it would level off. After either path [climb or level off] the program would execute the statement following end if.

64

This is still not a realistic approach to altitude control. With so many airplanes in the sky, the flight control system requires that airplanes fly at the altitude in the flight plan. The program must now be extended to lose altitude if the craft is too high.

Another if statement could be written after the if—then—else statement, but using a second if statement after the else in the if—then—else statement is a better way.

```
if CURRENT_ALTITUDE <  PLANNED_ALTITUDE then CLIMB ;
else if CURRENT_ALTITUDE >  PLANNED_ALTITUDE then DIVE ;
        else LEVEL_OFF ;
        end if ;
end if ;
```

Note that indentation is used to group the lines within the if—then—else statements. This technique is particularly useful in large, complex problems.

In the program segment above, the altitude checks are grouped together, but the statement is still a bit hard to follow.

b. ELSIF—THEN Clause

Ada allows another clause in the if—then—else statement, the elsif—then clause. The elsif allows the programmer to add a condition to the else clause.

General Format

```
if  <condition>  then  <statements>  ;
elsif  <condition>  then  <statements>  ;
        ——any number of elsifs may be used
else  <statements>  ;
        ——only one else is allowed
end if ;
```

Using elsif, the airplane altitude problem is written as follows:

```
if CURRENT_ALTITUDE < PLANNED_ALTITUDE then CLIMB ;
elsif CURRENT_ALTITUDE > PLANNED_ALTITUDE then DIVE ;
else LEVEL_OFF ;
end if ;
```

Using the elsif allows the programmer to write the altitude check much more clearly and simply. It is easier for someone who is not familiar with the program to understand what is being accomplished.

1. if X > Y then X := 22 ;
   end if ;
   Z := Y ;
   What is the value of Z if:

       a.   X = 7 and Y = 9
       b.   X = 7 and Y = 7
       c.   X = 13 and Y = 4

2. if 2 * [A + B] > C − 7 then Z := 14 ;
   elsif   B − C < A   then Z := 18 ;
   elsif   A * C > = B   then Z := 26 ;
   else   Z := 19 ;
   end if ;

   What is the value of Z if:

       a.   A = 7,   B = 16,   C = 9
       b.   A = 8,   B = 9,   C = 29
       c.   A = 9,   B = 14,   C = 7
       d.   A = 4,   B = 3,   C = 16

3. The "on" position of SWITCH_A is given the name HELD.

   Write the statements that sends the program to COMPUTE

   if SWITCH_A is off and to ROUTINE if it is on.

4. Triangles named A, B and C are of different sizes.
   Determine which is largest under the following conditions.

   a. A > B and A > C
   b. A > B and A < C
   c. A < B and B > C
   d. A < B and B < C

   Write the necessary control statements using A_BIG, B_BIG and
   C_BIG are flags of type Boolean. They are initialized to false and
   then assigned the value true when the condition is met.

5. Another part of the aircraft flight control program governs the speed
   of the aircraft. The optimum speed is 500 knots. Assuming there
   are engine control functions called MORE_ THRUST, LESS_THRUST
   and STEADY_THRUST, write the control statements to keep the airplane flying at 500 knots.

   If the speed drops below 100 knots, there is one engine function
   called FULL_THRUST which is used.

   Be sure to declare the variables of appropriate types.

CORRECT ANSWERS

1. a. Z = 9
    b. Z = 7
    c. Z = 4

2. a. Z = 14
    b. Z = 14
    c. Z = 14
    d. Z = 26

3. if SWITCH_A = HELD then ROUTINE ;
    else COMPUTE ;
    end if ;

4. A_BIG, B_BIG, C_BIG : Boolean := FALSE ;
    if A > B, A > C then A_BIG := TRUE ;
    elsif A > B, A < C then C_BIG := TRUE ;
    elsif A < B, B < C then C_BIG := TRUE ;
    elsif A < B, B > C then B_BIG := TRUE ;
    end if;

5. type AIRSPEED is delta .1 range 0 . . 1000 ;
    CURRENT_SPEED, PLANNED_SPEED : AIRSPEED ;
    begin
          PLANNED_SPEED := 500 ;

    if CURRENT_SPEED < PLANNED_SPEED then MORE_THRUST ;
    elsif CURRENT_SPEED > PLANNED_SPEED then LESS_THRUST ;
    elsif CURRENT_SPEED < 100 then FULL_THRUST ;
    else STEADY_THRUST ;

---

2. Case Statements

In some applications a great number of possibilities must be tested in order to choose the desired action. A lengthy elsif statement may be used, but this requires many tests. It is more desirable to make one test and to choose the action based on the result.

In this type of action the result cannot be binary since its value is not restricted to true or false, but to any of several different types of values. The case statement provides this capability.

General Format

```
case          < tested expression> is
      when <expression value>   =>      <statements>   ;
      --there may be any number of when clauses
      when others =>      <statements>   ;
end case;
```

Explanation:

case, is, when, when others, end case	— keywords required by the case statement
$\Rightarrow$	— symbol to indicate that the statements following will occur when the tested value is found to be true
<tested expression>	— may be anything that produces discrete values. It may be numeric or non-numeric ; character strings or other types
<expression values>	— the expression values must be constant values of the same type produced by the tested expression
when others	— may be used only once in a case statement, as it is the default case — the action to be taken when none of the others are true

If a tested expression is evaluated to a value not handled by one of the when clauses and the when others clause is not given, an error results. When the sequence of statements started by one of the case values is completed, the next statement executed is the one after end case.

Example

A program to count the number of different ways a football team scores. The values of possible scores are:

touchdown–6 points, extra point–1 point, field goal–3 points, safety–2 points

Any other value would be an error. The data would be a stream of integers representing the values of the scores as they occurred. The program would read a value, determine what kind of score it was and then increment the appropriate counter.

```
type COUNTER is range 0 . . 1000 ;
SCORE, TD, EP, FG, SAFETY : COUNTER ;
        .
        .
        .
TD      :=    0 ;      --initialize all counters to zero
EP      :=    0 ;
FG      :=    0 ;
SAFETY :=    0 ;
        .
        .
        .
case    SCORE is
        when 6 =>   TD := TD + 1 ;     --adds 1 to the TD counter
        when 3 =>   FG := FG + 1 ;     --adds 1 to FG counter
        when 2 =>   SAFETY := SAFETY + 1 ;
        when 1 =>   EP := EP + 1 ;
end case ;
```

What occurs in this little partial program is that the data is read into the variable SCORE, which then becomes the tested expression in the case statement. The value of the expression is the value of the variable SCORE.

If the value of SCORE is 3, then the counter incremented would be FG [field goal]. After the counter is increased, execution of the program continues at the first statement following end case.

Suppose the data to be evaluated for a team looks like this:

3 6 1 6 1 3 6 3 6 1 6 1 3 2 7 3

When the evaluation was completed, what would be the value of each counter ?

TD [touch down]   =   5
EP [extra point]   =   4
FG [field goal]   =   5
SAFETY   =   1
ERROR encountered with   7

In a case statement, only one of the conditions can be true since all < expression values must be distinct. In the if statement, the order of testing may be important, but in the case statement it makes no difference since only one condition can be true.

WORK AREA

1. In the football problem on the previous pages, if the TD counter stood at 5 and the EP counter stood at 4, how many points had been scored ?

2. The football problem case statement did not allow for an error number [such as the 7 in the example]. Write the portion of the case statement that would take care of such an error condition.

3. Write a case statement for counting the number of occurrences of the vowels A E I O U in a file of text containing only letters. Count the vowels separately and the consonents collectively.

4. A fraternity decides to have a beer tasting party to discover their favorite beer. They buy cases of Bud, Coors, Schlitz, Miller, Lowenbrau, Old Milwaukee, Pabst and Heinekin. The researchers voted for their favorites by entering the first letter of the brand name. Write a case statement [no pun intended] to count the votes.

CORRECT ANSWERS

1.   34 $-$ SCORE := 6 * TD + 1 * EP $-$ each TD is worth
                6 points and each EP is worth 1 point.

2.   when others =>   ERROR_ROUTINE ;

3.   case LETTER is
```
          when A =>      VOW_A := VOW_A + 1 ;
          when E =>      VOW_E := VOW_E + 1 ;
          when I =>      VOW_I := VOW_I + 1 ;
          when O =>      VOW_O := VOW_O + 1 ;
          when U =>      VOW_U := VOW_U + 1 ;
          when other =      CONS := CONS + 1 ;
       end case;
```
Prior to writing the case statements, VOW_A, E, I, O, U and CONS had to be defined to the name LETTER.

4.   case BEER of
```
          when B =>      BUD := BUD + 1 ;
          when C =>      COORS := COORS + 1 ;
          when H =>      HEINEKIN := HEINEKIN + 1 ;
          when M =>      MILLER := MILLER + 1 ;
          when O =>      OLD_MILWAUKEE := OLD_MILWAUKEE + 1 ;
          when P =>      PABST := PABST + 1 ;
          when S =>      SCHLITZ := SCHLITZ + 1 ;
          when others =>    BEER_ERROR ;
       end case ;
```

B. Character Strings

Using a variable which may contain only one character is often not practical, since characters are usually used in combination with others. A <u>character</u> <u>string</u> allows the programmer to use a single variable or constant to represent many characters. The character string is defined as a one-dimensional array of characters. [Arrays will be encountered in more detail later in the chapter.]

General Format

type STRING_TYPE_NAME is STRING (1 .. N) ;

N is the number of characters in the string and must be greater than 0 [zero].

Examples

```
type PAGE_LINE is STRING (1 . . 92) ;
type PERSON_NAME is STRING (1 . . 100) ;
type IO_BUFFER is STRING (1 . . 256) ;
```

Declaring string variables follows the familiar patterns as shown below:

```
FIRST_NAME : PERSON_NAME (1 . . 15) ;
INPUT_BUFFER : IO_BUFFER ;
```

Often string variables are declared using only the predefined type STRING ;

```
SCREEN_PROMPT : STRING (1 . . 80) ;
MANUFACTURER_NAME : STRING (1 . . 100) ;
NACL : constant STRING := "SALT" ;
WIFE_NAME : STRING (1 . . 20 ) :=  (4 . . 9 =    "SHARON") ;
```

Note that a string <u>literal</u> is enclosed in double quotes while single character literals [assigned to character variables] are enclosed in single quotes. There is a difference between 'A' and "A". The former is a character literal while the latter is a character string of length one. Attempting to compare 'A' to "A" would cause an error.

Several operations and relations are defined for string variables. Strings may be checked for order using the relational operators:

< less than	>= greater than or equal
<= less than or equal	= equal
> greater than	/= not equal

The use of these operators permits the sorting of lists of strings into alphabetical order.

WORK   AREA

1. What is the purpose of a character string ?

2. Declare a variable called FIRST which will encompass the first 22 positions of PAGE_LINE.

3. Write a type declaration for a character string called ENTRY containing 10 positions.

CORRECT ANSWERS

1. To allow the use of a single variable or constant to represent many characters.

2. PAGE_LINE : FIRST (1 . . 22) ;

3. type ENTRY is STRING (1 . . 10) ;

---

1. Comparing Strings

The order of the characters in the ASCII character set is shown in Appendix B. The order of the characters in the set is called the <u>collating sequence</u>.

For example, the digits 0 through 9 appear before the upper case letters A through Z, which appear before the lower case letters a through z. Thus the comparison '9' < 'A' is true, '8' < 'a' is true, 'A' < 'a' is true, 'A' < 'Z' is true, 'a' < 'z' is true.

The blank has the lowest position of all printable characters in the collating sequence. Blank is less than the special characters, digits, upper case and lower case letters.

Comparisons are done character by character until the strings are different or until one string ends.

Example

Compare the strings "BARBER" and "BARBELL"

Each position of the two strings would be checked until a difference is found or the strings are found to be of different lengths. The first five comparisons would be equal:

$$\begin{array}{ccccc} B & A & R & B & E \\ \downarrow & \downarrow & \downarrow & \downarrow & \downarrow \\ B & A & R & B & E \end{array}$$

The sixth comparison registers a difference:

Since 'R' comes after 'L' in the collating sequence, the relation is that "BARBELL" < "BARBER". In this case, the length of the character string does not determine the order of the strings, but if "BARB" was compared to "BARBELL", it would be lower because it had fewer letters.

It is possible to work with only parts of a character string, using <u>slices</u> of the array of characters. A slice is denoted by a range designation legal for the type.

Define strings with initial values:

SOURCE : STRING (1 .. 10) := (1 .. 8 =>   'BACKPACKER') ;
TARGET : STRING (1 .. 15) := (1 .. 15 =>   '*') ;
SHORT   : STRING (1 .. 6) := (1 .. 6 => ' '   ) ;

In computer memory these might be envisioned as follows:

SOURCE | B | A | C | K | P | A | C | K | E | R |

TARGET | * | * | * | * | * | * | * | * | * | * | * | * | * | * | * |

SHORT | | | | | | | |

Using the above strings, some assignments may be made:

TARGET (1 .. 3) := SOURCE (2 .. 4) ;
TARGET (5 .. 7) := SOURCE (6 .. 8) ;

After these assignments, TARGET would contain:

| A | C | K | * | A | C | K | * | * | * | * | * | * | * | * |

Assignments made to SHORT :

SHORT (3)   := TARGET (7) ;
SHORT (1 .. 2) := SOURCE (1 .. 2) ;
SHORT (4 .. 5) := SOURCE (9 .. 10) ;

This would result in SHORT containing: | B | A | K | E | R | | TARGET (7)
provided the 'K', SOURCE (1 .. 2) provided the "BA" and SOURCE (9 .. 10)
provided the "ER" to form the word "BAKER" in SHORT.

WORK   AREA

1. Using the strings and initial values given at the top of the page and the following assignments:

SOURCE (5 .. 8) := TARGET (1 .. 4) ;
TARGET (1 .. 3) := SHORT (1 .. 3) ;
TARGET (5 .. 7) := SOURCE (8 .. 10) ;
SHORT (2 .. 5) := SOURCE (5 .. 8) ;

a.   What will SOURCE contain ?

b.   What will TARGET contain ?

c.   What will SHORT contain ?

CORRECT ANSWERS

1. a.   SOURCE ⟶ | B | A | C | K | * | * | * | * | E | R |

    b.   TARGET ⟶ | | | | * | * | E | R | * | * | * | * | * | * | * | * |

    c.   SHORT ⟶ | | * | * | * | * | |

The portions of SOURCE that were changed when the first assignment statement was executed, stayed changed. There is no returning once a change has been made.

Comparing Strings continued

It is possible to make assignments using the same variable.

Example

Assume that | B | A | K | E | R | | was in SHORT:
SHORT (4 . . 6) := SHORT (3 . . 5) ;
The statement results in: | B | A | K | K | E | R |

There is an additive operator for strings called <u>catenation</u> which uses the symbol &. If A and B are strings, the operation A & B puts the first character of B immediately behind the last character of A.

Examples

A : STRING (1 . . 5) := "SUGAR" ;
B : STRING (1 . . 5) := "COOKY" ;
C : STRING (1 . .10) := (1 . . 10 => ' ') ;

C := A & B ;

The string variable C will now contain the value:
| S | U | G | A | R | C | O | O | K | Y |

C (1 . . 5) := A (5) & B (2 . . 5) ;

The above assignment results in the string "ROOKY" in the first five characters of string variable C. The last five characters of the variable C are unchanged.

76

1.　　A : STRING (1 . . 3) := "ADA" ;
　　　　B : STRING (1 . . 6) := "MANTLE" ;
　　　　C : STRING (1 . . 7) := (1 . . 7 =　"*") ;

What are the results in C of the following assignments.　Assume the problems are distinct;
C always starts with its initial value.

　　　　a.　　C (1 . . 7) := A & B (1 . . 4) ;
　　　　b.　　C (5 . . 6) := B (2 . . 3) ;
　　　　　　　C (3 . . 4) := B (5 . . 6) ;
　　　　c.　　C (2 . . 5) := A (1) & B (5 . . 6) ;
　　　　d.　　C (1 . . 5) := B (5) & A (1 . . 2) & B (5 . . 6) ;

2.　　D := STRING (1 . . 6) := "PLEASE" ;

Write assignment statements to put the string "EASEL" into string variable C defined
above.

3.　　Using string variable D above, put the string "SEALS" into
variable D, into the first five positions.

1.   a.   "ADAMANT"
       b.   "* * LEAN *"
       c.   "* ALE * * *"
       d.   "LADLE * *"

2.   C (1 . . 5) := D (3 . . 6) & D (2) ;

3.   This cannot be done simply by doing catenation.

       D (1 . . 4) := D (5 . . 6) & D (4) & D (2) ;

       The assignments are done left to right, so that when D (5 . . 6) are placed in the first two positions, the 'L' required for position 4 is replaced by an 'E'.

       Using a series of assignment statements, the desired result can be obtained.

       D (3) := D (4) ;
       D (4) := D (2) ;
       D (1 . . 2) := D (5 . . 6) ;

C. Composite Types

The simple numerical, Boolean, or character types, variables and constants that have been encountered thus far are adequate for solving most programming problems. However, many times a programmer must work with collections of related data which are not all of the same type.

It may be necessary to read a long list of measurements done by the same sensor, or it might be necessary to group logically related but physically different pieces of data together so that they may be manipulated as a unit.

Naming lists of similar values and grouping logically related data are the uses made of arrays and records.

1. Arrays

In previous examples, the input value read by the program is replaced by the next input value. However, many applications require that all the data items be kept so that they may be manipulated as a whole. One could declare a different variable for each data item, but this would be a cumbersome and unwieldly approach.

Suppose [for example] that some calculations are to be accomplished on the test grades of a class. If the class has only a few members [say five or so], it is easy to write a program using separate variables to determine the class average and to order the list in descending order. However, a similar program for a class of thirty or more becomes huge and unmanageable.

Example

```
procedure DO_GRADES is
        type GRADES is range 0 . . 100 delta .01 ;
        GRADE1, GRADE2, GRADE3, SUM, AVERAGE, GRADE_TEMP,
        HIGH_GRADE, LOW_GRADE : GRADES ;
begin
        NUM_GRADES := 0 ;
        SUM := 0 ;
        HIGH_GRADE := 0 ;
        LOW_GRADE := 100 ;
        get (GRADE1) ;
        get (GRADE2) ;
        get (GRADE3) ;
        -- calculate average grade
        AVERAGE := (GRADE1 + GRADE2 + GRADE3) / 3 ;
        put (AVERAGE) ;
        -- sort in descending order: GRADE1 will hold the highest
        -- value ; GRADE3 will hold the lowest value
        if GRADE1 < GRADE2 then   -- exchange 1 and 2
                GRADE_TEMP := GRADE2 ;
                GRADE2 := GRADE1 ;
                GRADE1 := GRADE_TEMP;
        end if ;
        if GRADE1 < GRADE3 then   -- exchange 1 and 3
                GRADE_TEMP := GRADE2 ;
                GRADE2 := GRADE1 ;
                GRADE1 := GRADE_TEMP ;
        end if ;
        -- GRADE1 should now contain the highest value
        -- next check to see that GRADE2 is second highest
        if GRADE2 < GRADE3 then   -- exchange
                GRADE_TEMP := GRADE3 ;
                GRADE3 := GRADE2 ;
                GRADE2 := GRADE_TEMP ;
        end if;
```

```
                -- the three grades should now be in descending order
        put (GRADE1) ;

        put (GRADE2) ;

        put (GRADE3) ;
end DO_GRADES ;
```

As it is written, this is not a good program because it is not easily extended. To handle four grades instead of three would require the addition of several lines of code including a major revision of the sorting process. Modifying the program to handle even thirty grades would result in 27 more variable names and several pages of additional statements to sort the scores.

Since all the scores are the same type and range, it is necessary to find a way of naming them with a single variable name yet retaining the ability to manipulate the individual elements. In mathematics, the vector is used to collect related values under one name, but allows its individual components to be used. Ada borrows the vector concept and modifies it to result in the array type.

In mathematics, the position in the vector of an element is denoted by its subscript. For example, if vector A has five elements they are denoted as a_1, a_2, a_3 a_4, a_5. In Ada, the same idea is used, referencing elements of the array by their subscripts. However, since most computers do not support physical subscripts, the subscript is put in parentheses after the array name.

Examples

A (3)   -- refers to the third element of array A

LONG (6)   -- refers to the sixth element of array LONG

The subscript [index] may be of any discrete type such as integer or enumeration type.

Simple Format of Array Declaration

type   type name   is array   < index range >   of   < component type >   ;

The index range may be specified in two ways. The range may be given in the same fashion as the range of the other types, giving the upper and lower limits of the range.

Example

type PRINT_LINE is array (1 . . 132) of CHARACTER ;

In this example, all variables declared to be type PRINT_LINE will have the same index range (1 . . 132), meaning that all arrays of type PRINT_LINE have exactly 132 components of type CHARACTER.

Declaring an array type with a specific index range is called a <u>constrained</u> array type declaration. The second way of declaring the index range is called the <u>unconstrained</u> array type declaration. This will be discussed on the following pages.

WORK   AREA

1.   What is the purpose of declaring an array ?

2.   Arrays and records are grouped under what type grouping ?

3.   What is a simple definition of the use of a vector ?

4.   How would one refer to:
      a.   array GO_AHEAD element 4
      b.   array SWITCHES element 12

5.   Write type declarations for the following:
      a.   Call the type REVERSE of BACK component with a range of 1 to 20.
      b.   Call the type AHEAD of component NOW with a range of 1 to 6.

1. to name lists of similar values for use in the program

2. composite types

3. to collect related values under a single name

4. a. GO_AHEAD (4)

   b. SWITCHES (12)

5. a. type REVERSE is array (1 . . 20) of BACK ;

   b. type AHEAD is array (1 . . 6) of NOW ;

---

a. Unconstrained Array Types

Often a program deals with many arrays of components of the same type but of widely varying size. It would be possible to determine what the largest array of that type would be and use that size in the type declaration. All array variables of that type would then be the same size [the same amount of computer memory would be reserved for each array).

This would be a poor method to use because many arrays would use only a small part of the range allotted to them. For example, a program might be written for the post office to process letters. Arrays might be used for the letters in the same town [which includes several zip codes], the same zip code [which includes many addresses] and for each address.

The town array would obviously be the largest and the address array the smallest although both deal with the same type of component, the letter. Declaring the array index range large enough to handle all the letters which are handled in a town might require a range of 50.

The unconstrained array type declaration is used under the type of condition described above, where arrays of the same type of components are needed, with varying sizes of index ranges. These are declared when the variables are declared.

General Format

type < type name > is array (index—type range < >) of < component type >

Example

The post office example might use a type declaration as follows:

type DESTINATION is array (INTEGER range 1 . . 1000_000 of LETTER ;
        TOWN : DESTINATION (1 . . 50_000) ;
        ZIP : DESTINATION (1 . . 5000) ;
        ADDRESS : DESTINATION (1 . . 50) ;

When the variable is declared and the array type is unconstrained, the constraint must be supplied with the variable declaration. See the following two pages for graphic examples of one, two and three dimensional arrays.

WORK   AREA

1. ANARRAY is a three dimensioned array of floating-point type items. The first dimension consists of six items, the second dimension of four items and the third dimension of two items. Call the dimensions INDEXA, INDEXB and INDEXC.

Write type and variable declarations for the above problem.

2. type QUAD is array (INTEGER range < > , INTEGER range < > ,
                INTEGER range < > , INTEGER range < >)
        of ELEMENTS ;
    DIM 4 : QUAD (2 . . 7, 1 . . 4, 11 . . 19, 0 . . 5) ;

How many elements are in the 4 dimensional matrix DIM4?

3. A two dimensional array type MATRIX is composed of fixed point numbers with a resolution of .25 and a range from −100 to +100. The indices are integers.

Declare the type.

Declare a variable BOX whose columns are indexed from 5 to 11 and whose rows are indexed from 89 . . 93.

83

CORRECT ANSWERS

1. INDEXA : INTEGER range 1 . . 6 ;
    INDEXB : INTEGER range 1 . . 4 ;
    INDEXC : INTEGER range 1 . . 2 ;
    type ANARRAY_TYPE is array (INDEXA, INDEXB, INDEXC)
        of digits 10 range −1E8 . . 1E8 ;
    ANARRAY : ANARRAY_TYPE ;

2. (7 − 2) x (4 − 1) x (19 − 11) x (5 − 0) = 5 x 3 x 8 x 5 = 600

    It is easy to declare an array which is bigger than all the storage available, so it is a good policy to be very careful.

3. type MATRIX is array (INTEGER < > , INTEGER < >)
        of delta .25 range −100 . . 100 ;

    BOX : MATRIX (89 . . 93, 5 . . 11) ;

Array Examples

1. one dimensional array

    type SINGE is array (1 . . 12) of ELEMENTS ;

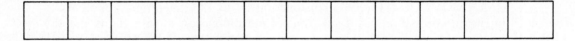

2. two dimensional array

    type DOUBLE is array (1 . . 7, 1 . . 8) of ELEMENTS ;

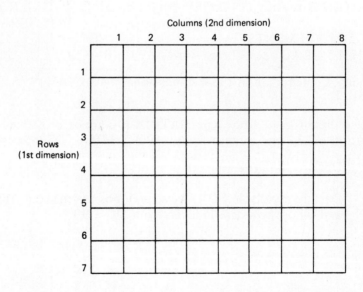

84

3. three dimensional array

    type **TRIPLE** is array (1 . . 6, 1 . . 5, 1 . . 3) of ELEMENTS ;

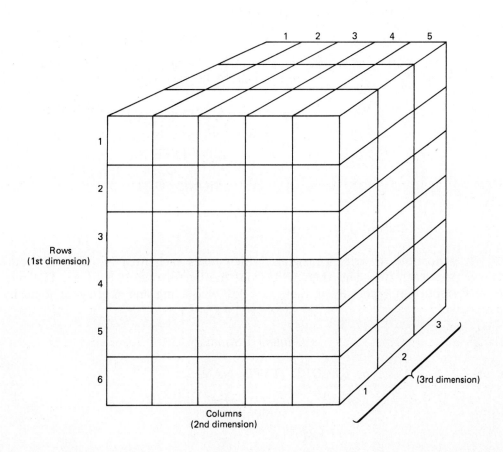

2. Records

Data of different types may be logically related. Consider [for example] a typical address book entry. It has a name, street address, city, state, zip code and phone number. In such an entry, the characters and integers are mixed thoroughly, but are logically related.

Example

typical entry	variable declarations
H. Chase	NAME : STRING (1 . . 25) ;
4045 Hancock St.	STREET_NO : INTEGER ;
San Diego, CA 92110	STREET_NAME : STRING (1 . . 20) ;
[714] 555-1011	CITY : STRING (1 . . 20) ;
	STATE : STRING (1 . . 4) ;
	ZIP : INTEGER ;
	AREA_CODE : INTEGER ;
	PHONE_NUM : INTEGER ;

a. Record Type Entries

It is possible to write a program which reads each item individually from a record, processes each item and then writes out each item one at a time. The record type is very important especially if there is a lot of reading and writing of logically related data.

General Format

```
type RECORD_TYPE_NAME is
     record
                component list
     end record ;
```

The component list is composed of variable and constant declarations, but not type definitions. A record may have nested record variables and may contain arrays as well. Using the address book entry from the example above, a record type can be declared as follows:

```
type ADDRESS_BOOK_ENTRY is
     record
             NAME : STRING (1 . . 25) ;
                _
                _
             [other entries as previously shown]
                _
                _
             PHONE_NUM : INTEGER ;
     end record ;
```

86

Declaring a record variable follows the familiar pattern, although the use of constraints and discriminants will be discussed in a later chapter. Record variables may be declared as follows:

PERSON : ADDRESS_BOOK_ENTRY ;
JOE : ADDRESS_BOOK_ENTRY ;

An array may be written:

BLACK_BOOK : array (1 . . 25) of ADDRESS_BOOK_ENTRY ;

WORK AREA

1. A program is to be written which will monitor a test of soft drinks which determines how many calories they have. The following information about each must be kept:

product name

sugar free or not

container size in ounces

calories per ounce

calories per container

Write a record type declaration for the above. Call it SODA.

2. Declare a variable of type SODA and call it TWELVE_OZ.

3. Declare a variable called CASE which is a 24 element array.

CORRECT ANSWERS

1. type SODA is
   record
           PRODUCT_NAME : STRING (1 . . 25) ;
           SUGAR_FREE : BOOLEAN ;
           CONTAINER_SIZE : OUNCES ;
           CALORIES_PER_OUNCE : delta .01 range 0 . . 1000 ;
   end record ;

2. TWELVE_OZ : SODA ;

3. CASE : array (1 . . 24) of SODA ;

---

b. Assigning Aggregate Values

Accessing the individual components of a record is different because of the composite nature of the record. It is no longer sufficient to simply say PERSON := 459 to assign a value to a record component. The individual component of the record to be used must be named, as in PERSON . STREET_NO := 459 ;

If it is desired to assign values to all [or some] components of a record, an aggregate of the component values may be used. If the aggregate values are in the same order as the components to which they will be assigned, the record assignment could be made as follows:

PERSON := ("HCHASE", 4045, "HANCOCK ST", "SAN DIEGO",
           92110, 714, 555 1011) ;

These values will be successively assigned to the variables in the record. This aggregate can be thought of as a positional aggregate, since the correspondence between data and variable is determined by their positions in the two lists.

It is possible to assign values to record components without putting them in order, but by associating the name of the component with the value to be assigned to it. Only the component name need be given, not the fully qualified component name [for example, PERSON : STREET_NAME]. The proper record is determined by the language from the left side of the assignment statement. This aggregate is called a named aggregate. It is useful if only a few fields at a time need to be changed.

A named aggregate assignment:

PERSON := (PHONE_NUM => 555 1100, AREA_CODE => 714,
          NAME => "J Wilt", STREET_NUM => 1709,
          STREET_NAME => "RAWLINGS ST", ZIP_CODE =>
          92119) ;

Note that all components have not been assigned values, but it is necessary for a record to have all fields used. An error will occur when all the fields of one record are assigned to another record if all the fields of the first record are not assigned values. However, assigning initial values to all the record components will ensure that the components always have some usable value.

A good way of accomplishing this is by specifying the values of the components in a new record. This is called <u>initialization</u> and should be done with all variables used in the program.

If initialization is not accomplished, it is possible for the fields that have not been given values to cause the program to produce distorted and erroneous results. Initializing will be discussed on the following pages.

WORK AREA

1. What are the two types of aggragates ?

2. In the previous section type SODA was declared, along with variables TWELVE_OZ and CASE. Using an aggregate assignment, assign these values to the variable TWELVE_OZ : TAB, 12 OZ, SUGAR_FREE, .75 calories per container, .0625 calories per ounce.

3. The 7th item in CASE has the following values:

    Name : DIET_SEVEN_UP, 16 OZ, SUGAR_FREE, 1 cal. per
           container, .0625 per oz.

    Write a positional aggregate assignment to put these values into the proper place.

4. Item 19 should be assigned the following values using a named aggregate:

    TOO SWEET, 12OZ, not sugar free, 400 calories per container, 33.333 calories per oz.

CORRECT ANSWERS

1. positional and named

2. positional aggregate:
    TWELVE_OZ := ("TAB", TRUE, 12, .0625, .75) ;
    or named aggregate:
    TWELVE_OZ := ("TAB", CONTAINER_SIZE => 12,
    SUGAR_FREE => TRUE_OUNCE, CALORIES_PER_
    CONTAINER => .75, CALORIES_PER_OUNCE => .0625) ;

3. CASE (7) := ("DIET SEVEN UP", TRUE, 16, .0625, 1) ;

4. CASE (19) := ("TOO SWEET", CONTAINER_SIZE => 12,
    SUGAR_FREE => FALSE,
    CALORIES_PER_CONTAINER => 400,
    CALORIES_PER_OUNCE => 33.333) ;

---

c. Initializing

To initialize a record component or variable, the assignment symbol is put after the component or variable declaration with the value to which the component or variable is to be initialized. Remember to initialize to a value in the variable range, but not normally expected as a value for the variable.

Examples

Record initialization:
```
type SHORT_ADDRESS is
    record
        NAME : STRING (1 . . 25) := (1 . . 25 => ' ') ;
                                    -- null string
        STREET_NUMBER : INTEGER := 0 ;
        STREET_NAME : STRING := "   " ;
        ZIP_CODE : INTEGER := 0 ;
    end record ;
```
Each time a variable of this type is declared it is automatically initialized. In effect, the type has been initialized.

It is possible to override the type initialization when a variable is declared by writing another initialization statement:

LISA : SHORT_ADDRESS := ("LISA SOHN", 1024, "VERMONT AVE", 92110) ;

90

It is possible to choose to change only a few fields:

JEFF : SHORT_ADDRESS := ("JEFF MENGEL", 762,
                          ZIP_CODE =>   92001,
                          STREET_NAME =>   "JASON") ;

In the previous example, the collection of values to be assigned to the record components [called an aggregate] combined positional association and named association. Positional association may be used until a named value is used, then all remaining values must be named.

A record aggregate may not have any "holes". All components must be given a value by either positional or named association.

Examples

LISA : SHORT_ADDRESS ; -- record variable declaration
LISA :- ("LISA SOHN", 1024, "VERMONT AVE", 92110) ;
LISA := (ZIP_CODE =>   92110, STREET_NUMBER =>   1024,
        NAME =>   "LISA SOHN", STREET_NAME =>   "VERMONT AVE") ;

The above two assignment statements fill the fields of the record variable LISA with the same values, although the fields are not filled in the same order.

_____

WORK   AREA

1. Write a record type to keep dates, to include month, day and year. Use 1900 to 2500 for the range of year. Be sure to initialize all fields.

2. Rewrite the declaration of type SODA with initializations of the record components. Remember that initial values should be values not normally expected. In this case, it is normal to expect zero calories in a drink, but probably not 1000 calories.

1. type DATE is
    record
        MONTH : INTEGER range 1 . . 12 := 0 ;
        DAY : INTEGER range 1 . . 31 := 0 ;
        YEAR : INTEGER range 1900 . . 2500 := 0 ;
    end record ;

2. type SODA is
    record
        PRODUCT_NAME : STRING (1 . . 25) := (1 . . 25 => " ") ;
        SUGAR_FREE   : BOOLEAN   := FALSE ;
        CONTAINER_SIZE: OUNCES   := 0 ;
        CALORIES_PER_OUNCE : delta .001 range 0 . . 1000 := 1000 ;
        CALORIES_PER_CONTAINER : delta .01 range 0 . . 1000 := 1000 ;
    end record;

---

d. Using Record Components

Aggregate assignments are useful for assigning values to several components, but often the programmer uses only one component at a time. It has been shown that using the record name is not specific enough. Naming the component must be more specific. In Ada, a <u>qualified</u> name is used to specify the component of the record to be used.

General Format

RECORD_NAME . COMPONENT_NAME

The qualified name must always have the record name first, then a period, followed by the component name.

Examples

1. Record type and record variable declared:

    type COMPLETE_DATE is
        record
            MONTH : STRING (1 . . 10) : = (1 . . 10 => ' ') ;
            DAY   : INTEGER range 1 . . 31 := 1 ;
            YEAR   : INTEGER range 1900 . . 2100 := 2100 ;
            TIME   : TIME_OF_DAY ;
        end record ;
    PAST : COMPLETE_DATE ;

A qualified name based on the record variable PAST may be used on either side of an assignment statement.

```
PAST . MONTH    := "MARCH" ;
PAST . YEAR     := 1982 ;
YESTERDAY       := PAST . DAY ;
LAST_YEAR       := PAST . YEAR ;
PAST . DAY      := 17 ;
```

2. Qualified names may also be used in other statements and as parameters to subprograms. This will be discussed in more detail at a later time.

```
if PAST . YEAR  < 1950 THEN IGNORE ;
ELSE TALLY ;
end if ;

case PAST . MONTH is
        when "JANUARY"      =>    WINTER ;
        when "FEBRUARY"     =>    WINTER ;
        when "MARCH"        =>    SPRING ;
end case
```

3. Records may contain another record as a component. In the declaration above, type TIME_OF_DAY may be a record declared as shown below:

```
type TIME_OF_DAY is
      record
                AM_PM  : (AM, PM) ;
                HOUR   : INTEGER range 1 . . 12 := 1 ;
                MINUTE : INTEGER range 1 . . 60 := 1 ;
                SECOND : delta .01 range 1 . . 60 := 1 ;
      end record ;
```

Component TIME of the previously declared type COMPLETE_DATE is a record of this type. Assigning values for the time in the variable PAST is done by extending the notion of qualified name, adding another period and the component name of the TIME record.

```
PAST . TIME . HOUR := 3 ;
PAST . TIME . HOUR := 17 ;
PAST . TIME . SECOND := 42.70 ;
```

There is no limit to this process although it quickly becomes cumbersome to use a variable name with many qualifications. One alternative is to use a variable local to the part of the program and assign the long qualified name to it.

Chapter 4 Summary

This chapter has introduced two of the three basic structures used in composing programs : sequence and conditional statements. The third [loops] will be covered in Chapter 5. Additionally, this chapter covers character strings and composite types [arrays and records].

Nearly all algorithms may be coded using the three structures [sequence and conditional statements and loops], although other language features may make the program easier to compose and understand. During the analysis of problems in preparation to the writing of programs, it is important to begin thinking in terms of these structures.

Chapter 4 Quiz

1.
```
procedure PGM is
    I, J, K : INTEGER := 1 ;
    LIM : constant INTEGER := 17 ;
begin
    while I < LIM loop ;
        I := I + J ;
        J := I + 2K ;
        K := J * I ;
        exit when K > LIM ;
    end loop ;
    put ( I ) ;
    put ( J ) ;
    put ( K ) ;
end PGM ;
```

   What values of I, J, K will be printed ?

2. A program which determines the latitude and longitude of towns is needed. The following information about each town will be used or altered: town name [up to 25 characters], county name [up to 25 characters], state [2 character abbreviation]. The position of the town consists of latitude degrees, minutes and seconds and longitude degrees, minutes and seconds.

   a. Write a type definition which can be used for all the data.

   b. Declare a variable and assign the values:

   latitude   35° 43′ 12″
   longitude 73° 27′ 42″

3. A program is to be written to manage the inventory of a book store. For each book, the following information is kept:

book title	the ISBN ident. number	cost
author name	copies on hand	selling price
publisher name	last order date	
publication year	no. of copies last ordered	

Name fields should allow at least 25 characters. The ISBN number is of the form 0 - 000 - 00000 - 0. [Divide into two parts, ISBN publisher and ISBN title.]

Declare a record type for this information and initialize it properly.

4. Based on problem 3, write variable declarations and assignment statements for the following two books:

> Principles of Software Engineering and Design
> Marvin V. Zelkowitz
> Alan C. Shaw
> John D. Gannon
> Prentice-Hall
> 0-13-710202-X
> published 1979
> copies on hand: 3
> last ordered: 4-28 this year
> no. copies ordered: 5
> cost: 18.95
> selling price: 24.95

> Software Development
> Clifford B. Jones
> Prentice-Hall
> last ordered: 6-8 last year
> no. copies ordered: 22
> published 1979
> 0-13-821884-6
> copies on hand: 2
> cost: 18.95
> selling price: 22.95

1. The exit when K > LIM will cause the loop to be exited when:

    I = 6   J = 18   K = 24

2. type POSITION is
        record
                DEGREES   : INTEGER range 0 . . 180 := 0 ;
                MINUTES   : INTEGER range 0 . . 60 := 0 ;
                SECONDS   : delta .01 range 0 . . 60 := 0 ;
        end record ;
    type TOWN_POSITION is
        record
                TOWN_NAME : STRING (1 . . 25) := (1 . . 25 := ' ') ;
                COUNTY_NAME : STRING (1 . . 25) := (1 . . 25 := ' ') ;
                STATE   : STRING (1 . . 2) :=   (1 . . 2 := ' ') ;
                LATITUDE   : POSITION ;
                LONGITUDE   : POSITION ;
        end record
    MY_TOWN : TOWN_POSITION ;

        —
        —

    MY_TOWN . TOWN_NAME := "SAN CARLOS" ;
    MY_TOWN . COUNTY_NAME := "RIVERSIDE" ;
    MY_TOWN . STATE   := "CA" ;
    MY_TOWN . LATITUDE . DEGREES := 35 ;
    MY_TOWN . LATITUDE . MINUTES := 43 ;
    MY_TOWN . LATITUDE . SECONDS := 12 ;
    MY_TOWN . LONGITUDE   := (73, 27, 42) ;

3. type BOOK_ENTRY is
        record
                TITLE : STRING (1 . . 25)   := BLANK25 ;
                AUTHOR : STRING (1 . . 25)   := BLANK25 ;
                PUBLISHER : STRING (1 . . 25) := BLANK25 ;
                PUB_YEAR : INTEGER range 1000 . . 2500 := 1000 ;
                ISBN_PUBLISHER : INTEGER range 0 . . 1000 := 0 ;
                ISBN_TITLE : INTEGER range 0 . . 100000 := 0 ;
                BOOKS_ON_HAND : INTEGER range 0 . . 2000 := 0 ;
                LAST_ORDERED : DATE ;
                COPIES_ORDERED : INTEGER range 0 . . 1000 := 0 ;
                COST : delta .01 range 0.0 . . 200.00 := 0 ;
                SELLING_PRICE : delta .01 range 0.0 . . 500.0 := 0 ;
        end record ;

4. The first thing the student should learn from this question is not to trust the specifications that are given without the benefit of real examples. Several fields will have to be lengthened and others added to the record.

Lengthen the string variables to 50 characters, increase the range of the ISBN fields to handle two more integer digits and add fields for a second and third author.

AUTHOR_2 : STRING (1 . . 50) := BLANK_50 ;

AUTHOR_3 : STRING (1 . . 50) := BLANK_50 ;

BOOK1 :=   ("Principles of Software Engineering and Design",
           "Marvin V. Zelkowitz", "Alan C. Shaw",
           "John D. Gannon", "Prentice-Hall",
           1979, 013,710202,3, (4,28,83), 5,
           18.95, 24.95) ;

BOOK2 :=   ("Software Development", "Clifford B. Jones",
           PUBLISHER => "Prentice-Hall", PUB_YEAR => 1979,
           ISBN_PUB => 013, ISBN_TITLE => 821884-6,
           BOOKS_ON_HAND => 2, LAST_ORDERED =>
           (6,8,1982), COPIES_ORDERED => 22,
           COST => 18.95, SELLING_PRICE => 22.95) ;

In addition to the two methods shown above this could also be accomplished in still another way:

BOOK2 . TITLE := "Software Development" ;

BOOK2 . AUTHOR := "Clifford B. Jones" ;

BOOK2 . PUBLISHER := "Prentice-Hall" ;

BOOK2 . PUB_YEAR := 1979 ;

—
—
—
—

5

LOOPS

LOOPS

A. GENERAL

Repeating a series of actions is often the major task of a computer program, whether it is to make periodic measurements as in an aircraft flight control program or counting the credits and debits of a bank account. The statement sequence could be written over and over again, but this would be tedious for the programmer and for large jobs might require more memory for instructions than the computer has available. In general, one also does not know in advance how many times an action will need to be repeated.

To provide the ability to repeat a statement sequence, Ada includes the loop construct, which may be named for convenience. If a loop is named, that same name must also appear after the end loop and before the semicolon.

General Formats

1. loop
    statement sequence ;
   end loop ;

2. LOOPNAME : loop
       statement sequence ;
   end loop LOOPNAME ;

The keywords are loop and end loop. Like the if and case statements loop must have a corresponding end loop. When the loop statement is encountered, the statement sequence is executed and when the end loop is reached, control returns to the loop statement and the statement sequence is repeated.

One typical use of the loop is to read in data, perform some work on it and repeat the action.

Example

Find the sum of integers in a file. An Ada program might be written as follows:

```
with TEXT_IO ;
procedure SUM_INTEGER is
        use TEXT_IO ;
        type MY_INTEGER is range 1000 . . 1000 ;
        INPUT_VALUE, SUM : MY_INTEGER ;

begin          -- keyword indicating the start of the procedure
        SUM := 0 ; -- initialize sum counter to zero
        loop
                get (INPUT_VALUE) ; -- read a value from the input file
                SUM := SUM + INPUT_VALUE ; -- add input to current
                -- value of SUM and put new value into SUM
        end loop ; -- control moves from here to top of loop
                put (SUM) ; -- writes the calculated sum to the
                -- output file
end SUM_INTEGER ; -- end of procedure
```

Explanation:

[1] The procedure is arbitrarily named SUM_INTEGER

[2] The statements with TEXT_IO and use TEXT_IO allow the use of the input and output statements get and put. These will be explained in more detail during later lessons.

[3] After declaring the types and variables, the implementation of the program begins with the reserved word begin.

[4] The first action taken is to initialize the variable SUM. It is necessary to know exactly where the accumulation of list values is to start and this is the reason for initializing SUM to zero immediately before beginning to add numbers to the list.

[5] Since the initialization is immediately before the loop statement, SUM is set to zero only once.

[6] Loop and end loop bracket the statements which are repeated. When the statements in the loop have been executed and the end loop is encountered, control is returned to the top of the loop, where the statement sequence is executed again. Each time through the loop a new value is read into INPUT_VALUE, then this value is added to the old value of SUM and this new value is assigned to SUM.

Looking at this program one soon discovers that the loop never ends. It continues to read and add data and it never reaches the put statement following the end loop. In practice, some type of error would halt the program, but this is certainly a very poor way to write a program [like designing a car with no brakes and stopping it by running into things].

WORK   AREA

1. What are the reserved words for a loop statement ?

2. In the example above:

   [a]   what is the name of the procedure ?

   [b]   what is the type ?

   [c]   what are the names of the variables ?

   [d]   where will the input data be placed ?

CORRECT ANSWERS

1.   loop   end loop

2.   [a]   SUM_INTEGER
     [b]   MY_INTEGER
     [c]   INPUT_VALUE, SUM
     [d]   into INPUT_VALUE

B. EXITING A LOOP

It is necessary to find a way to leave the loop when the action inside the loop is accomplished. There are several different ways to control a loop.

1. The exit when Loop

One exit method is to test a condition and leave the loop if the test result is true. To accomplish this, the exit when statement is added to the loop statement.

General Format

```
loop
      < statement sequence >   ;
   exit when   < condition >   ;
      < statement sequence >   ;
end loop ;
```

If the condition after the exit when is true then the next statement executed is the first one after end loop. The exit when statement may appear anywhere in the loop body: immediately after the word loop; immediately before the end loop or with other statements in the loop.

Example

```
loop                    loop                    loop
  — —                      exit when — — ;         — —
  — —                      — —                     — —
  — —                      — —                     exit when — — ;
  exit when — — ;          — —                     — —
end loop ;              end loop ;                 — —
                                                 end loop ;
```

2. Other Exit Methods

There are several ways to use the exit when statement in the list example shown on page 100,but knowledge of the data is required. One common way is to use a special data value to trigger the exit.

For example, if it is known that all of the data being summed is positive, then if a negative number is placed at the end of the input data and each value is tested until the negative value is found, the loop can be exited.

Example

Assume that the numbers in a file are as shown below with the addition of a −1 at the end of the file.

2 7 3 17 9 6 8 14 5 12 −1

Using the list example, the loop can be written as follows:

```
SUM := 0 ;
loop
      get (INPUT_VALUE) ;
      exit when INPUT_VALUE  <  0 ;
      SUM := SUM + INPUT_VALUE ;
end loop;
```

In this example, reading a new value and adding it to the sum continues until a negative value is encountered. The test is made before the sum is formed because the "tagged" value is not really part of the data to be worked on. When the test finds the negative value, the sum statement is skipped as control goes to the statement after end loop.

WORK AREA

```
loop
      < statement >   ;
      < statement >   ;
    exit when COUNT = 21 ;
end loop ;
```

After execution of the exit statement:

1. where will the program go if COUNT = 12 ?

2. where will the program go if COUNT = 21 ?

103

CORRECT   ANSWER

1. back to repeat the loop

2. to the next statement after end loop

---

3. The while and until Loops

The exit when loop provides a mechanism for doing a test and leaving
from anywhere in the loop.   Very often it is desirable to do the test at the beginning of the loop, before the statement sequence is executed.

This may be accomplished with an exit when loop, but another way to do
this is with the while loop.   The while loop also checks a condition and if true,
executes the statement sequence.   If false, it will go to the next statement after end
loop.

General Format

```
while    <condition>    loop
        <statement sequence>    ;
end loop ;
```

Since the condition test is first, the statement sequence would not be
executed if the condition tested were false initially.   If the exit when statement is
placed just before the end loop statement [following the statement sequence] the
loop statements are executed once before the condition is tested.   This type of
loop is called an until loop.

Format

while loop	until loop
while <condition> loop	loop
<statement sequence> ;	<statement sequence > ;
—	—
—	—
—	exit when <condition> ;
end loop ;	end loop ;

The while loop and until loop are the two basic logical loop structures.
All loops are in one or the other of these forms.   Ada has more physical loop
structures, but they all fit into these two logical types.

104

Examples

1. while loop

```
while not EMPTY loop
    if X (I)  <  1 and X (I)  >   −1
    then EMPTY := TRUE ;
    I := I + 1 ;
    end if ;
end loop;
```

2. until loop

```
loop                    -- X and Y are assigned initial values before the
    X := Y ;            -- loop is entered
    Y := Y + Y / 2 ;
    exit when ABS (X − Y)   < .005 ;
end loop ;
```

ABS is a built-in function which finds the absolute value.

WORK   AREA

1. Write a loop which reads characters one at a time into an array called BUFFER until a character called EOL [end of line] is encountered. Try writing it three ways: as a while loop, until loop and exit when loop.

2. An automatic weather monitoring station records temperatures every time there is a 1º or greater change. Temperatures can be in the range −100ºC. to + 100ºC. At the end of each 24 hour period the station writes a very large positive value to indicate end-of-day.

Write an Ada program which would read and average the temperatures in a 24 hour period.

CORRECT ANSWERS

1.

<u>while</u> loop

```
I := 0 ;
while not (CHAR = EOL) loop
     get (CHAR) ;
     I := I + 1 ;
     BUFFER (I) := CHAR ;
end loop ;
```

<u>until</u> loop

```
I := 1 ;
loop
     get (CHAR) ;
     BUFFER (I) := CHAR ;
     I := I + 1 ;
     exit when CHAR = EOL ;
end loop ;
```

<u>exit</u> <u>when</u> loop

```
EOLFOUND := FALSE ;
I := 1 ;
loop
     get (CHAR)
     if CHAR = EOL
     then EOLFOUND := TRUE ;
     end if ;
     exit when EOLFOUND ;
     BUFFER (I) := CHAR ;
     I := I + 1 ;
end loop ;
```

The EOL character will be stored in the buffer in the <u>until</u> loop.

2.

```
procedure DAILY_AVERAGE_TEMP is
     SUM, AVERAGE, COUNT, TEMP : delta .25 range -100 . . 1000 ;
     -- the upper limit of 1000 is used so the "tag" value will
     -- be valid for the type
begin
     SUM := 0 ;
     COUNT := 0;
     AVERAGE := -100 ;    -- not initialized to zero since zero is a
                          -- likely daily average
     loop
          get (TEMP) ;
          exit when TEMP  > 100 ;
          SUM := SUM + TEMP ;
          COUNT := COUNT + 1 ;
     end loop ;
     AVERAGE := SUM / COUNT ;
     put (AVERAGE) ;
end DAILY_AVERAGE_TEMP ;
```

4. End-of-File Condition

Using the previous looping methods required that a special condition be established and then tested. Whenever possible, a program should be very general so that it will fit all possible conditions that may be expected to appear, thus eliminating the need to make changes to the program.

In practice, changing an existing program is difficult because the person assigned to change the program is seldom the person who wrote the program. Most of the effort is spent learning how the program does its work and finding the proper spot to make the change.

Usually, the input values are processed until there are no more left in the file. At this point, the end-of-file has been reached. End-of-file is actually a special symbol placed at the end of the file to denote its limit. Symbolically, this could be shown as follows [assuming a section of magnetic tape]:

Beginning of file mark   13   7   9   6   22   17   2   29   End-of-file mark

In the Ada standard input/output package is a function which checks for the end-of-file mark each time a new item is read into memory. If the new item is the end-of-file mark, the function [called END_OF_FILE] returns the value True; otherwise it returns the value False.

The Standard input file is called input and the Standard output file is called output. The END_OF_FILE function should be given the file name used for input, such as END_OF_FILE [INPUT] ;

A function is actually a special kind of program which is called into action in an expression by its function name. Much more will be said about functions later in the text.

Using the while loop and the function END_OF_FILE, the earlier summation problem can be written as follows:

```
SUM := 0 ;
while not END_OF_FILE (INPUT) loop
    get (INPUT_VALUE) ;
    SUM := SUM + INPUT_VALUE ;
end loop ;
```

The not is a Boolean operator which gives the complement of the Boolean value it precedes. Not true is false, not false is true.

As previously stated, the while loop operates only when the test condition is true. In the example above, END_OF_FILE returns false for good data items. A not false value is evaluated to true and the loop statements are executed.

When the end-of-file is finally reached, the END_OF_FILE function returns true, but <u>not</u> <u>true</u> is evaluated as false, which sends control to the first statement following the end loop.

While this seems a bit contrived, it gives more generality which is desirable in writing reusable, easily maintained programs.

5. Counting Loop Executions

Counting the number of times the loop is executed is often found useful. For example, if it were desirable to calculate the arithmetic mean [average] of the values in the data file, it would be necessary to know the number of items in the file.

To count the data items, another variable of type integer is created, arbitrarily called COUNT. COUNT is then initialized to zero outside the loop and a statement which increments [increases] the variable COUNT is put after the summation statement.

When the loop is exited, COUNT will contain the number of times the loop statements were executed [which would also be the number of data items read]. After the loop, the average of the data items could be calculated.

Example

```
Procedure AVERAGE_A_FILE is
        type MY_INTEGER is range −1000 . . 1000 ;
        INPUT_VALUE, SUM, COUNT, AVERAGE : MY_INTEGER ;
begin
        SUM := 0 ; —— initialize SUM, that will accumulate the total
        COUNT := 0 ; —— initialize counter of number of items
        while not END_OF_FILE (INPUT) loop
                get (INPUT_VALUE) ; —— read new data item from file
                SUM := SUM + INPUT_VALUE : —— add new value to SUM
                COUNT := COUNT + 1 ; —— add 1 to count
        end loop ;
        AVERAGE := SUM / COUNT ; —— Although the formula is
                —— correct, the result will probably be wrong
                —— Why is that so?
        put (AVERAGE) ; —— write out the result
end AVERAGE_A_FILE ;
```

The result calculated for the average in this program will probably be wrong because the problem has been set up in the type INTEGER. With an integer type, fractional values cannot be represented. Since the result of the division most likely will not be integral, the remainder is truncated [dropped off] and only the whole number part is assigned to the integer variable.

Using actual numbers as an example:

[a]   assume the number of times through the loop was 22.

[b]   assume the total accumulated was 124.

COUNT will contain 22

SUM will contain 124

The formula is AVERAGE := SUM / COUNT

Dividing 124 by 22 results in 5.636, which [using rules of arithmetic] would be rounded up to 6. However, the strict integer arithmetic of Ada results in the truncation of the decimal fraction .636, leaving 5 as the result in AVERAGE.

WORK AREA

How could the program example on the previous page be fixed to eliminate the truncation problem?

CORRECT ANSWERS

There are several possibilities:

     1. A different data type could be used, such as floating point or fixed point for the variables. However, using "non-exact" numbers like fixed or floating can introduce errors, particularly if one desires to end when a variable takes on an exact value.

     2. Integers could be converted to a type which allows fractional parts. This is discussed in Section C below.

     3. Fixed point division could be simulated.

Example

     Suppose two decimal places of accuracy is desired. Multiply the dividend SUM by 100 and perform the division SUM / COUNT. Average would contain the value 563. To print the proper answer, divide 563 by 100 to get 5 [integer division] and print the 5, then print a decimal point. Multiply the 5 by 100 to get 500 and subtract from 563. Print the result to get 5.63, which is a fixed point result obtained by doing integer arithmetic.

C. Type Conversions

     Ada was designed to prevent type conversions from occurring without the programmer realizing that it happened. All type conversions in Ada must be done explicitly, so that no undetected mistakes are made.

     The conversion is accomplished by putting the variable to be converted in parentheses after the new type name.

NEW_TYPE_NAME (VARIABLE)

     For now, we will discuss conversion only between numeric types. Other conversions will be encountered later. The characteristics of the new type are superimposed on the old type, including range constraints.

     For the average example [originally shown on page 108], it is necessary to declare the variable AVERAGE to be of type real, or fixed point. Then the type name is used for the conversion.

Example

```
procedure AVERAGE_A_FILE is
        type MY_INTEGER is range −1000 . . 1000 ;
        type AV_REAL is digits 10 range −1000 . . 1000 ;
        SUM, COUNT, INPUT_VALUE : MY_INTEGER ;
        AVERAGE : AV_REAL ;
```

```
begin
    SUM := 0 ;
    COUNT := 0 ;
    while not END_OF_FILE loop
        get (INPUT_VALUE) ;
        SUM := SUM + INPUT_VALUE ;
        COUNT := COUNT + 1 ;
    end loop ;
    -- now for the explicit type conversion
    AVERAGE := AV_REAL(SUM) / AV_REAL(COUNT) ;
    put (AVERAGE) ;
end AVERAGE_A_FILE ;
```

The explicit conversions of SUM and COUNT from type MY_INTEGER to type AV_REAL allows the variable AVERAGE to be calculated with a fractional value.

The result of expressions may be converted, but care should be taken. Consider AV_REAL(SUM / COUNT). Is this the same as AV_REAL(SUM) / AV_REAL(COUNT)? The answer is no! In AV_REAL(SUM / COUNT), integer division occurs and fractional parts are truncated before the conversion takes place. In AV_REAL(SUM) / AV_REAL(COUNT) the integer types are converted to real and then divided using real number division, which preserves the fractional parts.

WORK AREA

1. Suppose SUM and COUNT were declared to be type INTEGER and have values 227 and 29 respectively. AVERAGE is declared; AV_TYPE is digits 6 range 0 . . 1000 ; AVERAGE : AV_TYPE ;

What is the value of AVERAGE for the following statements:

      a. AVERAGE := SUM / COUNT ;
      b. AVERAGE := AV_TYPE (SUM / COUNT) ;
      c. AVERAGE := AV_TYPE (SUM) / AV_TYPE (COUNT) ;

2. Type TAX_RATE is digits 10 range 0 . . 100 ;
   type DOLLARS is delta .01 range −100_000 . . 100_000 ;
   INCOME, TAX_OWED : DOLLARS ;
   RATE : constant TAX_RATE := .27984 ;

Write a statement which calculates TAX_OWED by multiplying INCOME by RATE, taking care to match types.

CORRECT ANSWERS

1. a. ERROR – type mismatch – an INTEGER may not be assigned
        to type AV_TYPE without conversion.
    b. AVERAGE = 7.000_000 – the integer division truncates the
        fractional part before the number is converted.
    c. AVERAGE = 7.8275862 – the integers are converted and real
        division is accomplished.

2. TAX_OWED := DOLLARS (RATE * TAX_RATE (INCOME)) ;
    Income is of type DOLLARS and must be converted to type
    TAX_RATE to be multiplied. This result is of type TAX_RATE
    and must be converted to DOLLARS to be assigned to
    TAX_OWED.

---

1. Meeting the Test Condition

Truncation can occur when real types are converted to integers or fixed
point. Truncation may occur when fixed point types are converted to integer types.
There may also be a small loss of accuracy when conversions are done due to the
different ways in which numeric types are represented in the computer.

For example, converting the value 5 from integer to real and back to
integer could result in a value like 4.9999999. Although this will not happen in
Ada for integers since the integer conversion process would produce the value 5
finally, loss of accuracy is a possibility when converting very large numbers or very
small numbers.

It is important to consider this possibility when testing for a particular
value. For example, if it is necessary to do something when X = 97.0, it may be
that because of the way X increases in the program, it will never be exactly 97.
The test would always fail and the program would be caught in an infinite loop.

In this example, the loop is never exited.

```
X := 0 ;
while (X / = 7) loop
      X := X + 2 ;
end loop ;
```

The variable X takes the values 2, 4, 6, 8, 10 . . . , therefore the exit condition is
never met and the loop continues indefinitely.

There are two ways to avoid this problem:

1] The loop condition can be changed to include a wider range of
    exit values.

    It could then be written:
    while not (X > = 7) loop

112

Variable X would take the values 2, 4, 6, 8. The 8 would trigger the exit because it satisfies the "greater than" part of the test.

> 2] Provide an error bound which includes values around the desired test value. For example:

```
Z := .4 ;
while not (Z = 4.3) loop
        Z := Z + .3 ;
end loop ;
```

Again, the loop would never terminate because Z would never take the value 4.3, but suppose that it is desired to leave the loop if Z is "fairly close" to 4.3. The "farily close" must be specified as to the acceptable error limits.

For example, if any value between 4.2 and 4.4 was accurate enough, it could be worked out as follows:

The mathematical relationship

$$4.2 \leqslant Z \leqslant 4.4$$

must be expressed in Ada. By subtracting 4.3 from each term, the following results:

$$- .1 \leqslant Z - 4.3 \leqslant .1$$

Mathematically, this is the same as writing:

$$| \ Z - 4.3 \ | \ < \ .1$$

where the vertical lines around $Z - 4.3$ mean <u>absolute value</u>.

(Absolute value always yields a positive result. It is defined:

$$\text{if } X \geqslant 0, \ | \ x \ | = X \qquad \text{or if } X \ < \ 0, | \ x \ | = -X$$

In Ada, vertical lines are not used, but there is a built in function called ABS, which returns the absolute value of the expression it is given.

The expression above says that if the difference between the variable Z and the value 4.3 is less than the predetermined allowable error .1, the condition is satisfied. This is written as:

```
Z := .4 ;
while ABS (Z - 4.3)   <= .1 loop
      Z := Z + .3 ;
   end loop ;
```

This loop does terminate when Z has the value 4.3. When Z is 4.3 the value of the expression is ABS (4.3 - 4.3) which is .0. This is less than .1.

D. Iterative Loops

Each trip through a loop is called an iteration. Iteration means repeated, successive activity. Many programs require repetition of some action a precise number of times. The programmer may do the incrementing of the loop counter [also called loop index], or the automatic incrementing feature of a loop may be used with an iteration clause.

Iterative Loop General Format

for   < loop counter >   in   < reverse >   < range >   loop
    < statement sequence >   ;
end loop ;

Unlike other variables in Ada, the loop counter variable does not have to be previously declared before use. However, the loop variable exists only during the loop and any attempt to reference the loop variable after the end loop statement will result in an error. The loop variable may not be modified by the programmer, but may be used in the loop as if it were a constant.

Example

For J in 2 . . 5 loop
    -- J exists only in the loop
    -- the for statement initializes, tests
    -- and increments loop counter J
end loop ;

The iteration statement causes the loop counter variable to be successively assigned all the values within the range. Since the loop counter variable is counting separate events, the variable must be of a type which is <u>discrete</u>. The most common discrete type is integer.

The integer loop counter is increased by one from the low value in its range until it is greater than the high value in its range. When the counter exceeds the upper limit of the range, the next statement to be executed is the first statement after the end loop statement. In the example above, the loop counter J would take the values 2, 3, 4, 5 and then the loop would be exited. The loop variable J exists only while the loop is being executed.

The loop variable [J*in the example] can never appear on the left side of an assignment statement. The for statement automatically takes care of the basic elements of any terminating loop:

---

*Note: Traditionally, programmers use names beginning with the letters I, J, K, L, M, N for loop counters and other integer counters. Ada does not require this practice, but if used consistently such a convention may be an aid in reminding a programmer for what a variable is used.

[a] a counter is initialized to a beginning value

[b] it is tested against the terminating value

      [1] if true [within the proper range], the loop statements are executed sequentially until end loop is reached, then control is returned to the top of the loop where the counter is incremented and then continues again through the loop

      [2] if not true [the counter exceeds the limit value], control goes to the first statement after end loop

The loop counter [also known as the loop parameter] can be used only indirectly as an index or on the right of an assignment statement. It may not be modified in any way within the loop. To use the value of the loop counter, it must be assigned to a declared variable. The variable may be modified, but this will not affect the loop counter.

WORK AREA

1. Using an iterated loop, write a statement sequence which sums the elements of an array with 14 elements called GAME.

2.
```
COUNT := 0 ;
for J in 7 . . 13 loop
    COUNT := COUNT + 1 ;
end loop ;
```
What is the value of COUNT when the loop is complete?

3.
```
COUNT := 0 ;
for K in 11 . . 22 loop
    COUNT := COUNT + K ;
    exit when COUNT  > 27 ;
end loop ;
```
What is the value of COUNT when the loop is exited?

4.
```
CIRCUITS := 0 ;
for M in −9 . . 7 loop
    CIRCUITS := CIRCUITS + 1 ;
end loop  ;
```
What is the value of CIRCUITS when the loop is complete?

5. In 2, 3, 4 above, of what type are J, K, M, the loop variables?

1.   SUM := 0 ;
                for I in 1 . . 14 loop
                        SUM := SUM + GAME (I) ;
                end loop ;

2.   COUNT = 7

3.   COUNT = 36

4.   CIRCUITS = 17   -- remember that M takes the value of zero

5.   Universal integer

Loop statements can be done manually by declaring the loop counter.

        J : INTEGER ;   -- the loop counter is declared
begin
        J := 2   -- initialize [J is assigned the value 2]
        loop
            exit when J > 5 ;   -- while J is less than or equal
                  –
                  –   -- to 5 continue looping
                  –
            J := J + 1 ;   -- increment J by 1
        end loop ;

Each manual loop causes loop counter J to take the values 2, 3, 4, 5 and to quit the loop when J gets to 6. The advantage of the automatic iteration is clarity and brevity. Mechanically there is no difference. Manual loops are dangerous because inadvertent assignments may change the loop counter and cause unexpected behavior.

The automatic and manual loop constructions are very similar, but each offers particular advantages in different situations. Unfortunately, it is not possible to make definite rules about when to use a particular form. Practice and experience give the programmer an intuition about which one to try first.

Generally, the automatic iteration is used when the entry and exit values are known and when the increment or decrement is one. The manual form of the loop is used when the exit condition is not based on the loop counter or when the increment or decrement is not 1.

Fibonacci numbers are formed by adding the two previous numbers to form the next number. Starting at zero, the Fibonacci numbers are

0, 1, 1, 2, 3, 5, 8, 13, 21, 34, 55, 89, etc.

Write an Ada program using a loop to produce the first twenty Fibonacci numbers. Print the numbers produced as they are calculated.

To keep the responses similar to the correct answer shown on the following page, use these names:

FIBONACCI_NUMBERS for the procedure
FIBONACCI for the type
NEW, LAST and BEFORE_LAST for the variables

This program is to print the values:
1, 2, 3, 5, 8, 13, 21, 34, 55, 89, 144, 233, 377, 610, 987, 1597, 2584, 4181, 6765, 10946. The initial values 0, 1 are not to be printed.

Print the value of NEW by using a put statement after the value of NEW is calculated.

CORRECT ANSWER

```
procedure    FIBONACCI_NUMBERS is
      type    FIBONACCI is INTEGER range 0 . . 100_000 ;
      NEW, LAST, BEFORE_LAST : FIBONACCI ;
begin
      BEFORE_LAST := 0 ;        -- initialize
      LAST           := 1 ;        -- with first two numbers
      for J in 1 . . 20 loop
             NEW := LAST + BEFORE_LAST ;
             put (NEW) ;
             LAST := NEW ;
             BEFORE_LAST := LAST ;
      end loop ;
end FIBONACCI_NUMBERS ;
```

In this answer, an automatically iterated loop has been used. Equivalent programs may be written using the manual forms of the loop.

E.   Nesting

Including one control structure within another is called _nesting_. It is possible to put an _if_ within a _loop_ or a _loop_ within an _if_. Most often, the term nesting refers to a loop within a loop.

Using loops within loops can cause an unexpectedly large number of statements to be executed. As an example, suppose that a three level set of nested loops are to be written to count the number of seconds in a day.

```
SECS := 0 ;
for HOURS in 1 . . 24 loop           -- 24 hours per day
      for MINUTES in 1 . . 60 loop -- 60 minutes per hour
            for SECONDS in 1 . . 60 loop -- 60 seconds per minute
                  SECS := SECS + 1 ;
            end loop ;
      end loop ;
end loop ;
```

Notice that each succeeding loop is indented and that the corresponding _end loop_ matches each _for_ at the same indentation. This technique allows one to quickly see the different loops. Good programmers have adopted this practice for clarity and understandability. It is a good technique for keeping track of nesting.

None of the numbers in the ranges of the three loops in the above example is very large, but the statement SECS := SECS + 1 is executed 86,400 times.

Note how the numbers grew so large: Each MINUTE loop causes the SECONDS loop to be executed 60 times. Each time the MINUTE loop completes its 60 iterations, the SECS := SECS + 1 statement has been executed 3600 times [the number of seconds in an hour]. The MINUTE loop is executed 60 times within each HOUR loop and each HOUR loop causes the MINUTES loop to be executed 24 times. When all the loops have been completed, the statement SECS := SECS + 1 has been executed 24 x 60 x 60 = 86,400 times.

Since loops cause the execution of a very large number of calculations, the programmer must take care to ensure that he does not use the nesting technique unnecessarily.

WORK AREA

Write nested loops to count the number of pennies in a dollar, considering the number of quarters per dollar, the number of nickels per quarter and the number or pennies per nickel.

To more closely resemble the correct answer, use the following names:

QUARTERS
NICKELS
PENNIES
CENTS for the counter

CORRECT ANSWER

```
for QUARTERS in 1 . . 4 loop
    for NICKELS in 1 . . 5 loop
        for PENNIES in 1 . . 5 loop
            CENTS := CENTS + 1 ;
        end loop ;
    end loop ;
end loop ;
```

The statement CENTS := CENTS + 1 will be executed 4 x 5 x 5 = 100 times.

Example of a 10 deep nest of loops:

```
for I1 in 1 . . 100 loop
    for I2 in 1 . . 100 loop
        for I3 in 1 . . 100 loop
            for I4 in 1 . . 100 loop
                for I5 in 1 . . 100 loop
                    for I6 in 1 . . 100 loop
                        for I7 in 1 . . 100 loop
                            for I8 in 1 . . 100 loop
                                for I9 in 1 . . 100 loop
                                    for I10 in 1 . . 100 loop
                                        - - -
                                        - - -
                                    end loop ; -- I10 loop
                                end loop ;        --I9 loop
                            end loop ;
                        end loop ;
                    end loop ;
                end loop ;
            end loop ;
        end loop ;              -- I3 loop
    end loop ;                  -- I2 loop
end loop ;                      -- I1 loop
```

The innermost statements of a 10-deep nest of loops which each go from 1 to 100 will be done 100,000,000,000,000,000,000 times. This is 1 million times the 1981 national debt of 1 trillion dollars.

Statements in nested loops are not confined to the innermost loop. They may appear before or after any nested loop. For example, counters could be added for minutes and hours in the example on page 118. This is an example of statements after a nested loop:

120

```
for HOURS in 1 . . 24 loop
        for MINUTES in 1 . . 60 loop
                for SECONDS in 1 . . 60 loop
                        SECS := SECS + 1 ;
                end loop ;
                MINS := MINS + 1 ;
        end loop ;
        HRS :=  HRS + 1 ;
end loop ;
```

The HRS counter is controlled only by the HOURS loop. It will be executed only 24 times. The MINS counter is directly controlled by the MINUTES loop and will be executed 60 times. Since the MINUTES loop is within the HOURS loop, the MINUTES loop will be executed 24 times, So the MINS counter will be executed 24 x 60 = 1440 times.

The following is an example of statements before a nested loop. Conditional statements are added to the example to check for particular times:

```
for HOURS in 1 . . 24 loop
        put (HOURS)
        if HOURS = 12 then put ('NOON') ;
        end if ;
        for MINUTES in 1 . . 60 loop
                if (MINUTES = 15) or (MINUTES = 45)
                        then put ("QUARTER_HOUR") ;
                elsif (MINUTES = 30) then
                        put ("HALF_HOUR") ;
                end if ;
        for SECONDS in 1 . . 60 loop
                SECONDS := SECONDS + 1 ;
        end loop ;
        MINS := MINS + 1 ;
        end loop ;
        HRS := HRS + 1 ;
end loop ;
```

These additional statements demonstrate a use of the loop counters within their loops.

The first if statement prints the word 'NOON' when the twelfth hour is reached. The test is made 24 times. The first if statement in the MINUTES loop prints the words 'QUARTER_HOUR' when MINUTES has either the value 15 or the value 45. Loop is performed 24 times, a total of 24 x 60 = 1440 times. The condition will be true twice for each performance of the MINUTES loop, or 48 times each day.
The next if statement prints the words 'HALF_HOUR' when MINUTES equals 30. This will be true once for each performance of the MINUTES loop, and 24 times each day.

WORK AREA

What messages will be printed every hour during a 24 hour period in the example above.

Each hour the following messages would print :

> QUARTER_HOUR
> HALF
> QUARTER_HOUR

at noon, it would print NOON, then QUARTER_HOUR, HALF, QUARTER_HOUR

Chapter 5 Summary

This chapter has introduced the third basic structure in the technique of program writing. The first two structures [sequence and conditional statements] were introduced in Chapter 4.

The work of the programmer is to translate algorithms in terms of statement sequences, conditional statements and loops. The system designer provides the programmer with information about the objects the programmer manipulates: data objects and the operations allowed on the data.

The allowed operations combine and transform the data and the algorithms which perform these operations are encoded by the programmer. In these early chapters, the work of the programmer is examined as it is related to the Ada language.

Chapter 5 Quiz

1. Assume that all variables are declared as integers in this Ada program fragment:

```
COUNT := 0 ;
for J in 3 . . 7 loop
    COUNT := COUNT + J ;
    for K in 2 . . 4 loop
        COUNT := COUNT - K ;
    end loop ;
    COUNT := - J * COUNT ;
    exit when COUNT  > 29 ;
end loop ;
put (COUNT) ;
    __
    __
    __
```

Chapter 5 Quiz, continued

a.   What value of COUNT will be printed by the put statement ?

b.   How many times is the <u>exit</u> <u>when</u> statement executed?

c.   How many times is the statement COUNT := COUNT – K
     executed?

2.   Write an Ada program to read a list of integers and determine the
highest and lowest values of the list. These values should be printed as well as the
number of integers that have been read.

3.   A small computer controls an underwater research craft. Part of the
program must continually check several measurements made by its sensors and perform appropriate actions:

a.   The current depth [the distance below the surface] is read and if it
     is 30 meters or more, the lights are turned on, otherwise they
     are off.

b.   If the current height above bottom is under 20 meters, the craft's
     legs are extended, otherwise they are kept retracted.

c.   The rate of descent is measured and if more than 10 meters per
     second, ballast is released to slow it, or if less than .25 meters
     per second, air is released to increase the rate of descent.

Write the appropriate type, variable and constant declarations and the Ada program
fragment to do these activities. Assume that the variables are available from the
standard input device.

CORRECT ANSWERS

1. a. 280
   b. once, but the condition is checked three times
   c. 9 times

2.
```
procedure MAX_MIN is
      MAX, MIN, THIS_VALUE :  range 0 . . 1000 ;
begin
      MAX := 0 ;          -- set MAX to lowest value
      MIN := 1000 ;       -- set MIN to largest value
      loop
           get (THIS_VALUE ) ;
           exit when (THIS_VALUE  > 1000) or (THIS_VALUE  < 1000) ;
           if THIS_VALUE    MAX then MAX := THIS_VALUE ;
           elsif THIS_VALUE  < MIN then MIN := THIS_VALUE ;
      end loop  ;
      put (MAX) ;
      put (MIN) ;
end MAX_MIN ;
```

3.
```
procedure SUB is
      type MEASURE is digits 10 range - 10_1000 . . 10_000 ;
      LIGHTS_ON : BOOLEAN ;
      LEGS_RETRACTED : BOOLEAN ;
      RELEASE_BALLAST, RELEASE_AIR : BOOLEAN ;
      CURRENT_DEPTH, RATE_OF_DESCENT,
                 HEIGHT_ABOVE_BOTTOM : MEASURES ;
begin
      LIGHTS_ON := FALSE ;
      LEGS_RETRACTED := TRUE ;
      RELEASE_BALLAST := FALSE ;
      RELEASE_AIR := FALSE ;
      loop
           get (CURRENT_DEPTH) ;
           get (RATE_OF_DESCENT) ;
           get (HEIGHT_ABOVE_BOTTOM) ;
           if CURRENT_DEPTH  > 30 then LIGHTS_ON := TRUE ;
           end if ;
           if HEIGHT_ABOVE_BOTTOM  > 20 then
                 LEGS_RETRACTED := FALSE ;
           end if ;
           if RATE_OF_DESCENT  > 20 then RELEASE_BALLAST
                 := TRUE ;
           else RELEASE_BALLAST := FALSE ;
           end if ;
           if RATE_OF_DESCENT  < .25 then RELEASE_AIR := TRUE ;
           else RELEASE_AIR := FALSE ;
           end if ;
      end loop ;
end SUB ;
```

6
SUBPROGRAMS

SUBPROGRAMS

A. General Purpose and Scope

In the previous chapters, the elements of Ada that are needed to write algorithms have been presented. Equally important to the software writer are the language features which allow the algorithms to be combined into systems. Ada was designed to produce large software systems and has several important features including subprograms, packages and tasks, which support the development of large systems.

The primary purpose of a subprogram is to allow repeated use of a particular algorithm or process withour having to rewrite the code for the algorithm each time it is needed. Subprograms provide a tool which allows an algorithm or process to be isolated within a well defined part of the software system. This allows errors to be found quickly and allows changes to be made more easily.

If the algorithm is sufficiently modularized, then changes to it can be made with less chance that unwanted side-effects will occur elsewhere in the system. The ideal subprogram appears to the rest of the program as a "black box," a unit whose internal structure and mechanism are unknown, but which performs a known process on the input to produce desired output.

The internal workings of the subprogram [how the data looks, its type, etc., or the algorithm employed] should be unimportant to the user; his interest is only in the result.

An example of a process which is often accomplished in the form of a subprogram is the sort. A sort produces an ordered list. To do this, a data object must be provided as input data and a compatible data object [for the sorted list to be output] must also be provided. The data objects may be [and often are] the same. To the part of the system which uses the sort, all that matters is that when the subprogram is given a list, it will return an ordered list. All the user of the subprogram needs to know is what type data object must be passed in and what will be returned.

B. Subprogram Structure

The structure of the Ada program units emphasize the difference between the interface and implementation of an algorithm. The interface part lists the information which goes in and out of the program unit and contains the descriptions of the data which are used in the program unit. The implementation part describes the algorithm by the use of language statements.

In Ada, the two parts may be written and compiled at different times. The software system can be totally described at the interface level and checked to see that the system design is complete and accurate before the working parts are written.

This may be compared to the building of a wooden mock-up of an airplane where the pieces are the same size as the pieces of the airplane [engine, instrument panel, controls, etc.]. This way, the way the pieces fit together [their interface] may be checked to fit. The working parts may then be constructed and fitted together with more assurance that it will work in the space allotted and with the adjoining pieces.

Abbreviated subprograms, called stubs, are used when implementing large systems. Stubs have an interface part, but initially the implementation part is only enough to satisfy the syntax requirements of the language. The process of successively adding the working body [implementation part] to the subprogram one at a time so that its effect on the system can be determined is called development by stepwise refinement.

Use of the stepwise refinement technique for creating software systems gives the programmer the facility to be able to determine if the implementation of the algorithm produces correct results and works within desired performance limits since only one small part has been added. If great, long programs are written, it is difficult to isolate where a problem is occurring without a detailed examination of the whole program.

WORK AREA

1. Name the two parts of a subprogram.

2. What is the purpose of each part ?

3. What is the purpose of a subprogram ?

4. What advantages are there in the use of subprograms ?

1. interface and implementation

2. interface lists the information needed and the implementation describes the working parts of the subprogram

3. to allow repeated use of a process or algorithm

4. errors are easily found and changes are easily made

C. Reducing Subprogram Size

One way of reducing the scope of concentration necessary in the development and checkout of programs is to limit the size of the problem one attempts to solve. Subprograms allow the programmer to solve small problems and isolate the solution. All the small parts are then fitted together to form the main system.

Subprograms may be of any length, but a good rule-of-thumb is to keep them to one page or about fifty lines. In that way, the whole subprogram is in front of the programmer when there is a problem, rather than forcing him to shuffle through several pages.

Holding to a fifty line limit forces the programmer to think the general problem through thoroughly enough to enable him to break it down into smaller problems. It must be remembered that this is just a rule-of-thumb [an easy way to adhere to a more general principle] and that there may be a need for exceptions in certain cases.

D. Types of Subprograms

There are two types of subprograms in Ada, the <u>function</u> and the <u>procedure</u>. The fundamental differences are the number of different values they return when used and the way in which the values are returned. A function returns one value only through the name of the function, while procedure may return zero to many values throughout parameters.

The two types are also brought into action in different ways. A function appears as part of an expression in a statement while use of a procedure is a separate statement. Both have the same general form of any Ada program unit, an interface part and an implementation part which may be separately compiled.

The procedure is the most general type of Ada subprogram. The procedure may receive data from the main program in the form of input parameters identified by the word <u>in</u> before the type name, perform some action and may pass data back to the main program in the form of output parameters identified by the word <u>out</u> before the type name. The subprogram algorithm is constructed using the parameters to represent the data which will be exchanged with the other programs which use the subprogram.

Example 2 on page 105 shows the use of a function in a program segment. The function is called by the use of the function name. Each time the name is invoked, the prescribed function is executed.

A subprogram that sorts a list of numbers may be written as follows:

```
procedure SORT (X : in out XARRAY ; N : in INTEGER)
        TEMP : INTEGER ;
begin
    for I in 1 . . N − 1 loop
        for J in I + 1 . . N loop
            if X (J)   <  X (J + 1) then
                TEMP := X (J) ;
                X (J) := X (J + 1) ;
                X (J + 1) := TEMP ;
            end if ;
        end loop ;

        end loop ;
end SORT ;
```

WORK AREA

Two arrays each contain 100 Social Security numbers. The arrays are sorted in ascending order. Merge the two arrays in order into a third array of length 200.

If SOC_SEC_A < SOC_SEC_B, then the third file gets the value of SOC_SEC_A. If this is not true, the third file gets SOC_SEC_B.

Write a subprogram which takes as input two arrays of sorted numbers and merges them into a third sorted array.

CORRECT ANSWER

```
procedure MERGE (X, Y : in SSARRAY ; Z out SSARRAY) is

— — —
I, J, K : INTEGER ;
— — —
begin
    I := 1 ; —— initialize counters
    J := 1 ;
    K := 0 ;
— — —
    while (I     = 100) and (J     = 100) and (K     = 200) loop
— — —
        if X (I)     = Y (J) then K := K + 1 ;
                                  Z (K) := X (I) ;
                                  I := I + 1 ;
        elsif X (I) = Y (J) then K := K + 1 ;        —— if elements are equal,
                                  Z (K) := X (I) ;    —— put both into Z and
                                  K := K + 1 ;        —— go on next in X and Y
                                  Z (K) := Y (J) ;
                                  I := I + 1 ;
                                  J := J + 1 ;
        else K := K + 1 ;
             Z (K) := Y (J) ;
             J := J + 1 ;
        end if ;
    end loop ;
— — —
    if I     = 100 then for N in J . . 100 loop
            K := K + 1 ;
            Z (K) := Y (N)
        end loop ;
    elsif J     = 100 then for N in 1 . . 100 loop
            K := K + 1 ;
            Z (K) := X (N) ;
        end loop ;
    elsif K     200 then put ("error —— Z array overflow") ;  NEW_LINE ;
    end if ;
— — —
end MERGE ;
```

---

1. Using a Subprogram Procedure

The subprogram procedure is considered to be an Ada statement. It may not be used in an assignment statement on either side of the assignment operator.

The name of the subprogram is written followed by its parameter list and a semi-colon. The use of the subprogram is said to be a <u>call</u>.

The parameter list in the subprogram call uses the <u>actual parameters</u> [the program data to be modified or used by the subprogram]. The traditional way of writing the parameter list is to list the parameters in the order they are described in the subprogram declaration and construction.

For example, in the SORT procedure on page 129, there were two formal parameters used: X [the array to be sorted] and I [the number of elements in the array]. In a program which reads in a list and then sorts it, the subprogram might be used as shown below:

```
procedure GET_AND_SORT is
     type INTARRAY is array (1 . . 100) of INTEGER ;
     LIST_LENGTH : INTEGER ;
     LIST : INTARRAY ;
          procedure SORT (X : in out INTARRAY, I : in INTEGER) ;
               TEMP : INTEGER ;
          begin -- this is the sort procedure described earlier
               while I >  1 loop
                    for J in 1 . . I - J loop
                         if X (J) <  X (J + 1) then
                              TEMP := X (J) ;
                              X (J) := X (J + 1) ;
                              X (J + 1) := TEMP ;
                         end if ;
                    end loop ;
                    I := I + 1 ;
               end loop ;
          end SORT ;
begin -- this is the implementation of GET_AND_SORT
     LIST_LENGTH :=    ;
     while NOT END_OF_FILE (INPUT) loop -- this loop reads in the elements
                                        -- of the list and counts them
          LIST_LENGTH := LIST_LENGTH + 1 ;
          get (LIST (LIST_LENGTH) ) ;
     end loop -- at this point the list is unsorted. The following is the call to the
              -- subprogram SORT
     SORT (LIST, LIST_LENGTH) ; -- the list is now sorted
                         -- the following loop will print the elements in order
          for I in 1 . . LIST_LENGTH loop
               put (LIST (I) ) ;
          end loop ;
end GET_AND_SORT ;
```

The subprogram call is the line SORT (LIST, LIST_LENGTH ;. The actual parameters are LIST and LIST_LENGTH, which take the place of the formal parameters X and I in the subprogram.

E. Procedures

A procedure is a more general case of the function. It may have any number of input parameters, but [unlike the function] the procedure may produce any number of outputs. The procedure call is a complete statement by itself, where the function call is part of an expression or statement. The procedure subprogram is used when more than one output result is required by a process.

Parameters may be defined as in, out, or in out. The meaning of each is as follows:

 a. An in parameter has its value used but not changed

 b. An out parameter passes data produced by the subprogram back to the calling program

 c. An in out parameter has the original value used and then [possibly] changed.

The parameters used to define the subprogram are called formal parameters.

Examples

1. procedure MAIN is . . . . .
    X : TYPEA ;
    Y : TYPEB ;
    Z : TYPEC ;
    procedure SUBPROGRAM (A : in TYPEA, B : in out TYPEB,
               C : out TYPEC) ;

      —
      —
      —

    begin —— SUBPROGRAM implementation
      —
      —
      —

    end SUBPROGRAM ;
      —
      —
      —

  begin — — — MAIN
      —

  SUBPROGRAM (X, Y, Z) ; —— Note that the procedure sub-
                —— program call is a complete
                —— statement by itself.
                —— X, Y, Z are actual parameters.

2. SUBPROGRAM (X, B ⇒ Y, C ⇒ Z) ; —— this is also a valid
      —— procedure subprogram call, using named parameter
      —— association rather than positional parameter association
  end MAIN ;

In the previous example it may be seen that the procedure subprogram is specified in the declaration part of the main procedure. The subprogram declaration includes both the subprogram interface/declaration part and the implementation part.

Parameters may be passed in two ways:

    a.   by putting the actual parameters in the same order as the formal parameters were used in the subprogram declaration; this is called <u>positional</u> <u>parameter</u> <u>passing.</u>

    b.   by indicating the association between formal and actual parameters using the symbol => , which is called <u>named</u> <u>parameter</u> <u>passing.</u>

The methods are logically equivalent; that is, there is no difference in the effect of the subprogram. For subprograms with a few parameters, the positional parameter passing method is normally used.

Ada permits the programmer to give default values to the formal parameters so that actual parameters need not be specified. In this case [where default values are used for parameters] named parameter passing is used to indicate which formal parameters are being replaced by actual parameters.

Once <u>named</u> <u>parameter</u> <u>passing</u> is used in a subprogram call, <u>positional</u> parameters may not be used after the <u>named</u> parameters. Named and positional parameters may be mixed, but the positional parameters always precede the named parameters [on the left].

WORK AREA

1. A program called MAIN has a procedure called SWAP which takes two integer parameters [called ALPHA and BETA] as input, exchanges the values and returns the values as output parameters.

    a.   Write the main program declaration part and include the subprogram declaration for SWAP.

    b.   In the body of the main program, write a subprogram call to SWAP which exchanges the values of ALPHA and BETA. Make sure that the two variables are declared properly.

2. If a variable (TEMP) is declared in the subprogram SWAP above, can it be directly used in the main program? Why?

3. True or False. Data declared in the main program can be used by a subprogram only if passed as parameters.

CORRECT ANSWERS

1. procedure MAIN is
        ALPHA, BETA : INTEGER ;
        procedure SWAP (P : in out INTEGER, Q : in out INTEGER) is
                TEMP : INTEGER
        begin
                TEMP   := P ;
                P   := Q ;
                Q   := TEMP ;
        end SWAP ;
    begin
        _
        _
        SWAP (ALPHA, BETA) ;
    end MAIN ;

2.   No — A variable declared in the subprogram is available to only that subprogram [or other subprograms declared within that one].

3.   False — The variables are available to the subprogram because the scope of the main program includes the subprogram [in this case]. Beware of the use of global variables in subprograms. Good programming style is to always use parameters to transfer data in and out of the subprogram.

If a variable is declared in the subprogram with the same name as a variable in the main program, the subprogram declaration "hides" the main program declaration. The main program variable may be used by preceding the variable name with the main program name.

Example

procedure MAIN is
    A : ATYPE ;
    procedure SUBPROG (X : in out ATYPE) is
        A : ATYPE ;
    begin
        A := X ; —— this A is the one declared in the subprogram
        _
        _
        MAIN . A := X ; —— this is the A declared in the main program
        _
        _
    end SUBPROG ;
begin   —— MAIN program
    _
    _
    _
end MAIN ;

134

Summary

This chapter introduces subprograms as a valuable programming tool. The major purpose of subprograms is to allow repeated use of a process or algorithm. It provides for easy recovery of errors and simplification in the making of changes to the program.

Parameters are used to define subprograms and to pass information in and out of the procedure or function.

The mode of the parameter describes how the data may be used by the procedure. In parameters are referenced only, in out parameters reference and change the data brought in, out parameters export new data.

If a subprogram is called from another subprogram, the parameter modes must match in the nested call.

CHAPTER 6 QUIZ

Write a program which concatenates two lists to make a third list. The source lists are of any length, up to 50 elements and elements have integer values between 1 and 1000.

Define types, declare variables and write the algorithm.

Assume values are input using a function GETL which is used by specifying the name of the list to be filled with values such as GETL (MY_LIST) ;

Determine the length of each list and print the length.

Each of the source lists is terminated by a zero value element or when the list is filled.

135

```
procedure  CONCAT_LISTS is
     type LIST is array (INTEGER range  <  >  ) of INTEGER range 0 . . 1000 ;
     SOURCE1,  SOURCE2 : LIST (1 . . 50) ;
     TARGET : LIST (1 . . 100) ;

     type LENGTH is new INTEGER range 0 . . 100 ;
     SOURCE1_LENGTH, SOURCE2_LENGTH, TARGET_LENGTH : LENGTH ;

     begin
     - - initialize variables and lists
     SOURCE1_LENGTH := 0 ;
     SOURCE2_LENGTH := 0 ;
     GETL (SOURCE1) ;
     GETL (SOURCE2) ;

     for I in 1 . . 50 loop
          exit when SOURCE1 (I) = 0 ;
          TARGET (I) := SOURCE1 (I) ;
          SOURCE1_LENGTH := I ;
     end loop ;

     for I in 1 . . 50 loop
          exit when SOURCE2 (I) = 0 ;
          TARGET (SOURCE1_LENGTH + I ) := SOURCE2 (I) ;
          SOURCE2_LENGTH := I ;
     end loop ;

     TARGET_LENGTH := SOURCE1_LENGTH + SOURCE2_LENGTH ;

     PUT (SOURCE1_LENGTH) ;
     PUT (SOURCE2_LENGTH) ;
     PUT (TARGET_LENGTH) ;
end CONCAT_LISTS ;
```

7
PACKAGES

PACKAGES

A. Introduction

Packages are the key structures for creating software systems in Ada so that complexity can be more easily managed. This is one of several large steps forward in the development of programming languages. Packages allow the grouping of logically related declarations, data and operations. Packages may be used to logically and physically isolate specific activity using certain specific data. This is called encapsulation.

Systems design, using data objects is encouraged by packages which allow both data and operations on the data to be defined. The information in a package must be explicitly accessed by a program unit. The information in packages can only be accessed if procedure, task, or other program element specifically requests the package by name. This ensures that the programmer does not accidentally change data.

The two phrases "with TEXT_IO ;" and "use TEXT_IO ;" call the package TEXT_IO into availability. TEXT_IO is a predefined package which allows the programmer to read and print data. It provides the basic input/output (I/O) functions GET and PUT and various other I/O related routines.

Through the Ada overloading capability, these functions are defined for the various Ada types which may be printed:

> integer, real, fixed point, character, string, enumeration type

Overloading allows the use of the same function name to read or write information of any type.

Examples

PUT ('X') ;	where X is a character
PUT (3) ;	where 3 is an integer

The TEXT_IO specification is an example of a large Ada package that uses several advanced features of Ada [such as generic procedures and functions which will be briefly described later in the book].

Within the package specifications are types, procedures, functions, other packages and exceptions. The package specification contains only the interfaces of the various I/O functions and procedures, but nothing about their implementation.

The ideal way to use a package is to put into the specification part [of the package] only that information which the programmer wants to make available and to hide the implementation details in a separate implementation part.

In the case of TEXT_IO this is necessary because the implementation of the TEXT_IO procedures and functions are largely dependent on the host computer system and will likely be very different for different computer systems.

For example, an IBM 370 computer uses a 32 bit word and represents characters in EBCDIC [Extended Binary Coded Decimal Interchange Code], a CDC Cyber uses a 60 bit word and has a unique internal character code, while a great many 16 bit minicomputers use the ASCII code to represent characters.

Although the algorithms for implementing a PUT or GET may be quite different on different systems, the programmer should not be required to understand such <u>machine</u> <u>dependent</u> <u>characteristics</u>. He only needs to know that PUT will cause something to be written and GET will cause something to be read.

Being able to assume that PUT and GET cause the same results no matter what computer system is used is important for writing programs which may be moved from one system to another with a minimum of changes. Separating the interface specification of the functions and procedures from their implementation allows this to happen.

WORK AREA

1. What is encapsulation?

2. How does a programmer call a package into use in his program?

3. What is the purpose of the Ada overloading capability?

4. When using a package, what does the programmer do with the two program parts: specification and implementation?

CORRECT ANSWERS

1. the isolation of specific activities from other activities in a program

2. by calling for its unique name using <u>with</u> or <u>use</u>

3. to allow the use of the same function to perform a similar operation for data of other types

4. keeps the two parts separated and hides the implementation details from the information in the specification segment

---

B. General Examples

Like any Ada program unit, the package has two parts: specification and implementation. The public part of a package may contain types, use clauses, constants, variables, subprogram declarations, other packages or tasks in any combination. Only information in the public part may be exported; private data [to be discussed later] or declarations made inside the implementation part are not available to program units which use the package. The simplest form of package collects related data [variables or constants] or type declarations. This data would be used as a common data base for several parts of a large system.

Example

The screen of a CRT can typically contain 25 lines of 80 characters each. Several different parts of a software system might alter the screen image, so each would need access to the data item representing the characters on the screen.   A package could be created called SCREEN_IMAGE. The basic format uses the key words: package NAME is

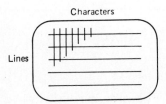

Fig. 7−1.   CRT Screen

```
package SCREEN_IMAGE is
     SCREEN_CHARS : constant INTEGER := 80 ;
     SCREEN_LINES : constant INTEGER := 25 ;
     type SCREEN_TYPE is array (INTEGER range  <   > , INTEGER
          range  <   > ) of CHARACTER ;
     SCREEN : SCREEN_TYPE (0 . . SCREEN_CHARAC − 1,
                             0 . . SCREEN_LINES − 1) ;
end SCREEN_IMAGE ;
```

140

The package SCREEN_IMAGE has only an interface part since there are no functions or procedures to be implemented. It contains a type definition and the declaration of two constants and a variable. By using the constants to represent the rows and lines on the screen the declaration of SCREEN is made more general and what the numbers 80 and 25 represent becomes obvious.

In the following variable declaration:

SCREEN : SCREEN_TYPE (0 . . 24, 0 . . 79) ;

the numbers 24 and 79 seem unusual and it is not obvious what they represent. The use of descriptively named constants clarifies the relationship of the array bounds to the array and it is then obvious what must be changed if a new CRT screen is 66 lines by 132 characters wide.

Example

If the CRT is being used in a word processing system, three different parts of the word processing software would modify the screen:

1. the text entry software would echo the characters input on the keyboard on the screen,
2. the file retrieval software would put part of a file on the screen for editing,
3. the formatting program would move text around on the screen as it indents, paginates, justifies, etc.

The three procedures can be named:

KEYBOARD   GET_FILE   FORMAT

If all three are separate main procedures, the programmer would import the package SCREEN_IMAGE [previous example] in the same way for each one, by using a with clause.

1. with SCREEN_IMAGE ;   2. with SCREEN_IMAGE ;   3. with SCREEN_IMAGE ;
    procedure KEYBOARD is   procedure GET_FILE is   procedure FORMAT is

    — — —   — — —   — — —

    begin   begin   begin

    — — —   — — —   — — —

    end KEYBOARD ;   end GET_FILE ;   end FORMAT ;

The with clause makes available to the program unit it precedes everything in the interface part of the package. In the case of SCREEN_IMAGE, a type, two constants and a variable are available.

To use the package contents in the program unit, the programmer must use a fully qualified name, that is, the package name followed by a period and the item name.

fully qualified name = PACKAGE_NAME . ITEM_NAME ;

Example

```
with SCREEN_IMAGE ;          -- Note:  no use clause for package SCREEN_IMAGE
procedure KEYBOARD is        -- fully qualified names must be used
     SCREEN_BUFFER : SCREEN_IMAGE . SCREEN_TYPE
                     (0 . . SCREEN_IMAGE . SCREEN_CHARAC - 1,
                      0 . . SCREEN_IMAGE . SCREEN_LINES - 1) ;
     CHAR, LINES : INTEGER ;
begin
     _ _ _

     SCREEN_IMAGE . SCREEN (CHAR, LINE ) := NEXTCHAR ;
          _ _ _

     if  LINE > = SCREEN_IMAGE . SCREEN_LINES then
          CHAR := CHAR + 1 ;
          if CHAR > = SCREEN_IMAGE . SCREEN_CHARAC then
               SCROLL_UP (1, SCREEN_IMAGE . SCREEN) ;
               - - SCROLL_UP moves text up the screen and leaves a blank line
               - - at the bottom
          end if ;
     end if ;
     _ _ _

end KEYBOARD ;
```

In this example a new variable has been declared called SCREEN_BUFFER using the type in SCREEN_IMAGE and the two constants.

In the implementation part of the procedure, an assignment is made to the variable SCREEN in the package, two comparisons using the constants are accomplished and a procedure call [using the variable] is made.

C. The Use Clause

Using qualified names can become tedious and cumbersome, so Ada provides a capability to do away with the qualification in the form of the use clause. The use clause makes all the items in the package directly visible to the program element. This means that the names of the items may be used without prefixing the package name.

Example

```
with SCREEN_IMAGE ;
procedure KEYBOARD is
use SCREEN_IMAGE ;
     _ _ _

begin
     _ _ _

end KEYBOARD ;
```

r

142

Note that the use clause is written after the title line of the program element. Note also that when the use clause has been included, the with clause must also be included. Use does not replace the need to include the with statement.

The use clause allows the programmer to use the item in the package without the qualifying package name. If several packages are accessed and all include the use clause, there is a danger of name conflict. If the same names are used in different packages then the names should be fully qualified when used [to alleviate the ambiguity].

Example

Package ALPHA might have a variable named THETA and package GAMMA might also have a variable named THETA. If procedure PGM uses both packages:

```
with ALPHA, GAMMA ;
procedure PGM is
use ALPHA, GAMMA ;
    — — —
begin
        — — —
        THETA := X ;
        — — which THETA is being used ?
    — — —
end PGM ;
```

Depending on the type of variable X the reference to THETA may be ambiguous, since the programmer could have meant either the THETA in ALPHA or the THETA in GAMMA. If both were the same type as X, there would be no way to resolve the identity of X. For this type of conflict, the fully qualified name must be used [in the above example, either ALPHA . THETA or GAMMA . THETA].

The programmer must carefully consider possible name conflicts before applying the use clause. The more packages which are accessed, the more name conflicts may arise.

The effect of the use clause on the example given on the previous page is shown on the following page. The use of the names is much less cumbersome, but the source of the items is obscured. Do not automatically include a use clause.

WORK   AREA

1. They keyword "with" is used for what purpose?

2. If the keyword "use" is used, what other keyword must also be used?

3. Given the following NOTATION : SEGMENT . SEG_TYPE ;
    which is the package name?

4. Where is the use clause always written?

5. What does the use clause permit the programmer to do?

CORRECT ANSWERS

1. to make available the interface of the package.
2. with
3. SEGMENT
4. after the title line of the program
5. use any item in the package without using the fully qualified name

---

Example

```
with SCREEN_IMAGE ;
procedure KEYBOARD is
use SCREEN_IMAGE ;
    SCREEN_BUFFER : SCREEN_TYPE (0 . . SCREEN_CHARAC-1,
                                 0 . . SCREEN_LINES-1) ;
    CHAR, LINE : INTEGER ;
begin
    _ _ _
    SCREEN (CHAR, LINE) := NEXTCHAR ;
    _ _ _
    if LINE  > = SCREEN_LINES then
        CHAR := CHAR + 1 ;
        if CHAR > = SCREEN_CHARAC then
            SCROLL_UP (1, SCREEN) ;
            _ _ SCROLL_UP moves text up the screen and leaves a blank line
            _ _ at the bottom of the screen
        end if ;
        _ _ _
    end if ;
    _ _ _
end KEYBOARD ;
```

It is plain to see from this example that the use clause allows the items in the package to be used just as if they were declared within the program unit.

D.   Collecting Related Entities

Packages can also be used to collect procedures, functions and other packages which are logically related. In this type of package the subprogram interface description [the line with the subprogram name and its parameter names and modes] is placed in the package interface, also called the "visible part." The implementation of the function or procedure is done in the implementation part of the package, called the package body.

Like the interface specification and implementation parts of procedures, the two parts of a package may be separately compiled. This capability is important when designing large systems since the "fit" of the parts of the systems may be checked by determining if the interfaces are consistent with each other.

The separate compilation of the specification and implementation parts of a package allows the algorithms implementing the procedures and functions to be changed or replaced [such as fixing an error] without having to change the rest of the system. For students writing short programs this may not seem important, but for huge systems which may have taken several years to develop it is very important to be able to make changes without unexpected side effects such as requiring other programmers to change other parts of the program.

1. A Stack

As an example of a package which collects related procedures, functions and data, consider the data object known as the stack. A stack may be logically compared to a physical stack in many ways.

In some cafeterias a special cart is used to hold plates. This cart has a spring system which keeps just one plate available at all times, just above the top surface of the cart, whether there is one plate remaining or a hundred.

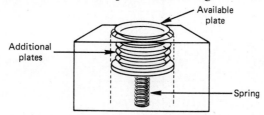

Fig. 7−2 − Plate Holding Cart

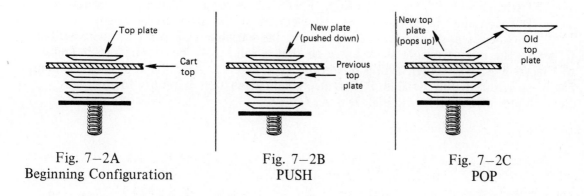

Fig. 7−2A
Beginning Configuration

Fig. 7−2B
PUSH

Fig. 7−2C
POP

In a stack, after a plate has been added or removed, the spring adjusts the stack so that only the top plate is available. Placing a new plate on top of the stack is called a push and removing a plate is called a pop.

2. Computer Representation of a Stack

In a computer, one way to represent a stack is with a one dimensional array. Each element of the array is an element of the stack. [This would correspond to the plates of the physical model. It may be helpful to imagine that each plate contains an element of information.]

Instead of a spring, a variable is used to keep track of the top of the stack. The top of the stack holds the last stored piece of data, which also is the next available piece of data. This is called last-in-first-out use of data [abbreviated LIFO].

Push is a data entry operation which adds to the stack and pop is a data retrieval operation which removes from the stack. One cannot pop an empty stack, nor can one push a full stack.

Symbolically, the PUSH and POP configuration may be represented as shown in Fig. 7—3 below.

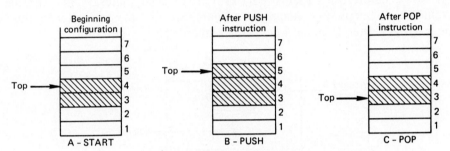

Fig. 7—3 — Symbolic PUSH and POP Configurations

The stack is represented by a linear array called STACK, indexed from 1 to STACK_ENTRIES [where STACK_ENTRIES is some constant]. A variable called TOP contains the index of the last element of the array to be filled.

When a push operation is necessary, the variable TOP must be incremented to get to the next available stack entry so that a value may be assigned to it [refer to Fig. 7—3 A, B]. When a pop operation is performed, after the top stack element has been accessed, the variable TOP is decremented so that it points to the stack element just below [refer to Fig. 7—3 A, C].

3. PUSH Procedure and POP Function

A procedure to perform the push operation must increment variable TOP and then assign a value to the array element pointed to by TOP. If a stack of integers is assumed, the push procedure would be written:

```
procedure PUSH (NEWDATA : in INTEGER) is
begin
      TOP := TOP + 1 ;        -- move TOP up one element
      STACK (TOP) := NEWDATA ;
                              -- assigns new value to top of stack
end PUSH ;
```

A procedure is used for push because it returns no value. Notice that variables TOP and STACK are not passed as parameters to the procedure. This is because these variables were declared at the same level as [or at a higher level than] the procedure. When this is true the scope of the variable contains the scope of the procedure and the procedure may use the variable without importing it as a parameter.

The pop operation is written as a function because it returns a value. The function decrements the variable TOP and then returns the top element of the stack before TOP was decremented. Here again, because variables TOP and STACK are treated as global variables to the function, no parameters are passed to the function.

Function POP could be written:

```
function POP return INTEGER is
      T : INTEGER
begin
      T := STACK (TOP) ;       -- get top value
      TOP := TOP - 1 ;         -- move top down
      return T ;               -- return value
end POP ;
```

In POP the value at the top of the stack is moved to a temporary holder. T. After the pointer to the top of the stack has been moved down one position, the value of the old top item is returned.

PUSH and POP operate on two variables, TOP and STACK which would be declared as follows:

```
      STACK_ENTRIES : constant INTEGER := 25 ;
      TOP : INTEGER range 0 . . STACK_ENTRIES ;
      STACK : array (1 . . STACK_ENTRIES) of INTEGER ;
```

The constant STACK_ENTRIES determines the size of the stack and can be changed as required. The range of variable POP allows the value zero although zero is not a legal index of stack.

TOP must be allowed to have value zero since PUSH adds 1 to TOP before assigning a value to the stack element. If TOP started at 1, stack element one would never be used since TOP adds 1 [to 1] and starts in the second element.

If the program attempts to PUSH a full stack the range of TOP will be violated and an error will occur. In the same manner, if the program attempts to POP an empty stack the range of TOP is violated and an error will occur.

The data TOP and STACK are logically related to the operations PUSH and POP and are ideal for packaging. There are several ways these items might be arranged in the packages with different effects. The following is one approach:

```
package OPEN_STACK is
        STACK_ENTRIES : constant INTEGER := 25 ;
        TOP : INTEGER range 0 . . STACK_ENTRIES ;
        STACK : array (1 . . STACK_ENTRIES) of INTEGER ;

        procedure PUSH (NEWDATA : INTEGER) ;
        function POP return INTEGER ;
end OPEN_STACK ;

package body OPEN_STACK is
        procedure PUSH (NEWDATA : INTEGER) is
        begin  -- PUSH
            TOP := TOP + 1 ;
            STACK (TOP) := NEWDATA ;
        end ;
        function POP return INTEGER is
        begin    -- POP
            TOP := TOP - 1 ;
            return STACK (TOP + 1) ;
        end POP ;
begin          -- OPEN_STACK
        TOP := 0 ; -- initialize TOP to zero
end OPEN_STACK ;
```

This version of the package exports the variables TOP and STACK and the operations PUSH and POP.

WORK AREA

1. The two parts of a package may be separately compiled. Why is this an important feature?

2. What are the two action features of a stack?

3.   a.   What is LIFO?

      b.   What does it mean?

4.   a.   Which operation adds to the stack?

      b.   Which operation removes from the stack?

5. What keeps track of the last element to be filled with data?

6. Why is a PUSH written as a procedure and a POP as a function?

1. allows changes to be made without affecting the rest of the system

2. PUSH and POP

3. a. last-in-first-out

   b. the last stored piece of data becomes the next available piece of data

4. a. PUSH

   b. POP

5. TOP

6. PUSH is a procedure because it returns no value and POP is a function because it does return a value

---

E. Information Hiding

A program unit which accesses the package OPEN_STACK [in the previous example] would be able to use any of the four items [TOP, STACK, PUSH, POP] as desired. However, allowing direct access to the data items can lead to unnecessary dependence on their implementation characteristics and allows the programmer to alter the variables without using the expected operations.

If TOP is modified other than with a PUSH or POP, it may make some of the stack information difficult to access or it may have uncertain validity. For this reason, it may be desirable to "hide" the information about how the stack is implemented and the variables which are used.

1. One Method

One way of information hiding in packages is to make data private. This effectively hides the implementation method. The reserved word private is used as shown in the example below. The type name may be exported to other program units and variables of that type used, but operations on private types are restricted to assignment, comparison for equality, or user defined operations made available in the same package.

Assume that a variable called STACK is declared to be private. This means that a user of the package knows there is a variable called STACK and that the operations allowed on it are assignment and comparison.

However, since the type of the private variable is not known to the programmer, assignment can take place only between variables of the same private type.

Example

```
package EXAMPLE is
     type STACK_TYPE is private ;
     MY_STACK, YOUR_STACK : STACK_TYPE ;
private          —— EXAMPLE
     STACK_ENTRIES : constant INTEGER := 25 ;
     type STACK_TYPE is array (1 . . STACK_ENTRIES) of INTEGER ;
end EXAMPLE ;
```

Two variables are declared, MY_STACK and YOUR_STACK. All that is known about these variables to a user of the package is that the variables are of type STACK_TYPE. If this package is used by a procedure, the variables can be used only in a very limited way.

Example

```
with EXAMPLE ;
procedure SMALL is
use EXAMPLE ;

begin
     if MY_STACK /= YOUR_STACK then     ——legal uses of the variables
          MY_STACK := YOUR_STACK ;
end SMALL ;
```

The only operations currently defined for the private type are assignment and comparison. In this case, trying to compare the two variables is logically meaningless. Also the built-in comparison operator is not defined for array comparisons so an error would result.

WORK AREA

1. What reserved word is used in packages to cause information to be hidden?
2. What operations are allowed on a private variable?
3.
```
     with EXAMPLE ;
     procedure PROB3 is
     use EXAMPLE ;
     A, B, C : STACK_TYPE ;
     begin     —— PROB3
          if A = B then A := C ;     —— a.  Is this legal?
          end if ;
          PUSH (A, 3) ;               —— b.  Is this legal?
          POP B ;                     —— c.  Is this legal?
     end PROB3 ;
```

CORRECT ANSWERS

1. private

2. assignment and comparison

3. a. this is legal —— comparison and assignment are defined for private types

   b. and c.
   these are not legal because procedures PUSH and POP are not defined in a package imported by procedure PROB3

Illegal Statements

1. MY_STACK (3) := YOUR_STACK (4) ;
   —— the type of the variable is not visible so array subscripting cannot be
   —— used – it is not known whether the stack is implemented as an array
   —— or not

2. MY_STACK := MY_STACK + 7 ;

   —— the + operator has not been explicitly defined for the private type –
   —— it would have to be defined as a function operating on the type

3. MY_STACK := MY_STACK * YOUR_STACK ;

   —— this is illegal because the multiply operator is not defined for this
   —— type – it would have to be defined as a function

Use of the private type is important to information hiding because it hides the implementation details of the data and restricts the operations on the type. The operations are restricted to the degree that the programmer must define them himself, requiring him to thoroughly understand the problem and to plan the solution before attempting the coding.

2. Overloading ; Second Method

In Ada, it is legal to redefine operators such as:

$$+, -, *, /, <, >, =$$

for user defined types. Using the same symbol for similar operations on different data types is called overloading.   The basic arithmetic and comparison operators are already overloaded in Ada, since it is permitted to add, subtract, etc., etc., real numbers, integers, or fixed point numbers with the same operator symbols.

The language processor automatically identifies which version of the operation is to be used by the type of the operands that are to be used.

Functions and procedures which act on private types are declared and defined as for any other type. The implementation of the subprogram must know how the private type is implemented.

The private type implementation is visible only in the package body, therefore the subprogram implementation must be done there. The subprogram interfaces must be stated in the package interface if they are to be available to other parts of the program.

Adding the operations PUSH and POP to the package EXAMPLE would be accomplished as shown on the following page :

Example

```
package NEW_EXAMPLE is
     type STACK_TYPE is private ;
     MY_STACK, YOUR_STACK : STACK_TYPE ;
     type STACK_ITEM_TYPE is private ;
     STACK_ITEM : STACK_ITEM_TYPE ;

     procedure PUSH (S : in out STACK_TYPE ,
                     SI : in STACK_ITEM_TYPE) ;
     procedure POP  (S : in out STACK_TYPE ,
                     SI : out STACK_ITEM_TYPE) ;
     private          -- NEW_EXAMPLE
         STACK_ENTRIES : constant INTEGER := 25 ;
         type STACK_ITEM_TYPE is INTEGER ;
         type STACK_PTR_TYPE is new INTEGER range 0 . . STACK_ENTRIES ;
         type STACK_TYPE is array (1 . . STACK_ENTRIES) of
                     STACK_ITEM_TYPE ;
end NEW_EXAMPLE ;
package body NEW_EXAMPLE is
        TOP : STACK_PTR_TYPE ;
        procedure PUSH (S : in out STACK_TYPE,
                     SI : in STACK_ITEM_TYPE) is
        begin     -- body NEW_EXAMPLE
                TOP := TOP + 1 ;      -- increment STACK_PTR_TYPE
                S (TOP) := SI ;       -- put new data on top of stack
        end PUSH ;
        procedure POP (S : in out STACK_TYPE,
                     SI : out STACK_ITEM_TYPE) is
        begin
            SI := S (TOP) ;           -- put data from top of stack into
                                      -- return parameter
            TOP := TOP - 1 ;          -- move top of stack down one element
        end POP ;
begin     -- package initialization
    TOP := 0 ;   -- top of STACK_PTR at bottom of stack
end NEW_EXAMPLE ;
```

Explanation of the previous example:

In the package NEW_EXAMPLE, the operations PUSH and POP have been added for the private data types STACK_TYPE and STACK_ITEM_TYPE. The implementation characteristics are well hidden from a user of the operations.

The type names describe the abstract qualities and logical purpose of the data, but give no clue to its physical description. Thus the package user can PUSH or

POP the stack and use the data items in it without knowing [or caring] if the stack is an array, or linked list, or tree, or other data type.

Similarly, the data items can be numbers or characters in an array, records in a linked list or in a tree, or something else. As long as the programmer is allowed controlled access to the data types through the defined functions, the actual data types and implementation of the operations may be changed with little or no change to the user's program.

In the package NEW_EXAMPLE, the procedures PUSH and POP act on data passed as parameters. Using parameters to explicitly pass data into a procedure is a good practice because it denotes to all users which data is to be used and altered and helps avoid unexpected side effects.

Only the assignment and comparison operations are allowed on the data types STACK and STACK_ITEM_TYPE. For example, two variables of STACK_PTR_ TYPE may be compared and the value of one may be assigned to the other, but no arithmetic operations have been defined so the variables could not be used for arithmetic.

Similarly, assignment and comparison are defined for STACK_ITEM_TYPE, but no other operations are allowed. No operations are defined which mix STACK_PTR_TYPE and STACK_ITEM_TYPE as operands [i.e., they may not be compared, assigned, or have arithmetic performed on them].

WORK AREA

What is the value of Z in the following?

```
with NEW_EXAMPLE ;
procedure HMAYER is
use NEW_EXAMPLE ;
    A, B, C : STACK_TYPE ;
    X, Y, Z : STACK_ITEM_TYPE ;
begin
    for I in revers 1 . . 10 loop
        PUSH (A, 2 * I + 1) ;
        PUSH (B, 13 − I) ;
    end loop ;
        POP (A, X) ;
        POP (B, Y) ;
        PUSH (C, X + Y) ;
        −
        POP (A, X) ;
        POP (B, Y) ;
        PUSH (C, X + Y) ;
        −
        POP (B, X) ;
        POP (A, Y) ;
        PUSH (C, X + Y) ;
        POP (C, Z) ;
end HMAYER ;
```

CORRECT   ANSWER

Z is 17

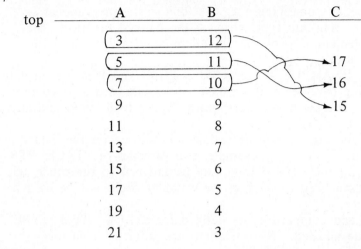

top	A	B	C
	3	12	17
	5	11	16
	7	10	15
	9	9	
	11	8	
	13	7	
	15	6	
	17	5	
	19	4	
	21	3	

3.   Third Method

The implementation characteristics of data may be hidden in another way, by placing them in the package body. There are subtle differences in packages constructed in this fashion.

These differences will be discussed after presenting the example below:

Example

```
package NEXT_EXAMPLE is
     procedure PUSH (NEW_DATA : INTEGER) ;
     function POP return INTEGER ;
end NEXT_EXAMPLE ;

package body NEXT_EXAMPLE is
     STACK_ENTRIES : constant INTEGER := 25 ;
     STACK : array (1 . . STACK_ENTRIES) of INTEGER ;
     TOP : INTEGER range 0 . . STACK_ENTRIES ;
     procedure PUSH (NEWDATA : in INTEGER) is
     begin          -- PUSH
         TOP := TOP + 1 ;
         STACK (TOP) := NEWDATA ;
     end PUSH ;

     function POP return INTEGER is
     begin          -- POP
         TOP := TOP - 1 ;
         return STACK (TOP + 1) ;
     end POP ;
begin                     -- body NEXT_EXAMPLE
     TOP := 0 ;   -- initialize to bottom of stack
end NEXT_EXAMPLE ;
```

156

Explanation:

This version of the package allows the programmer to store integers in a stack [unlike the previous example, which stored STACK_ITEM_TYPE). Access to the stack is limited to the operations PUSH and POP which add and retrieve integers to the stack.

The variable TOP is not available to the program part which uses the package. It is local to the package body and available only to the subprograms implemented in the package body.

In the previous package [NEW_EXAMPLE] the variable TOP of STACK_PTR_TYPE was available to the program using the package for assignment and comparison with variables of the same type.

Of the three packages illustrated, the second hides implementation information the best. The user deals only with abstract data types. Only the logical qualities of the data are available to the programmer.

The operations PUSH and POP put STACK_ITEMS, not integers, records, etc., on a STACK, whose implementation is also unknown. A variable of type STACK_PTR points to the TOP of the stack.

How TOP is implemented is unimportant to the package user; whether it is an array index, or an access variable, or something else. All the user needs to know is that TOP points to the top of the stack.

When the details of implementation are hidden, the user deals with a data object which has only well defined qualities and operations, with nothing implicitly known [such as if the data were known to be numeric or character].

F. Grouping Information

One use of the package in developing the software system is to group the information about a data object. This would include logical data types and associated operations.

Often in developing the software system design, it is adequate in the initial stages to describe only the logical properties of data and operations and to leave the actual implementation until later.

Because the system is implemented a little at a time, it is useful that the temporary descriptions of operations be legal in the language so that the compiler does not reject references to these temporary representations, called stubs.

Stubs of operations are the interface of the subprograms — the name and parameter list. They represent everything the user of the operation needs to know about the operation.

The operations PUSH and POP put STACK_ITEMS, not integers, records, etc., on a STACK, whose implementation is also unknown. A variable of type STACK_PTR points to the TOP of the stack.

How TOP is implemented is unimportant to the package user; whether it is an array index, or an access variable, or something else. All the user needs to know is that TOP points to the top of the stack.

When the details of implementation are hidden, the user deals with a data object which has only well defined qualities and operations, with nothing implicitly known [such as if the data were known to be numeric or character].

Example

In the package NEW_EXAMPLE, it is desired to use stubs for the operations PUSH and POP. The interface part of the package would be unchanged, but the package body would be as follows:

```
package body NEW_EXAMPLE is
      procedure PUSH (S : in out STACK_TYPE,
                              T : in out STACK_PTR_TYPE,
                              SI : in STACK_ITEM_TYPE) is
                              separate ;
      procedure POP     (S : in out STACK_TYPE,
                              T : in out STACK_PTR_TYPE,
                              SI : out STACK_ITEM_TYPE) is
                              separate;
begin              -- body of NEW_EXAMPLE
      TOP := 0 ;
end NEW_EXAMPLE ;
```

By stating that PUSH and POP are separate, they are termed subunits, which may be written and compiled later on.

1.   Compiling Subunits

When the subunits are to be compiled, they must be preceded by the phrase:
                            separate (parent_name)
where parent_name is the name of the package from which they were originally separated.

Examples

```
separate (NEW_EXAMPLE)
procedure PUSH   (S : in out STACK_TYPE,
                        T : in out STACK_PTR_TYPE,
                        SI : in STACK_ITEM_TYPE) is
begin      -- PUSH
      T := T + 1 ;
      S (T) := SI ;
end PUSH ;

separate (NEW_EXAMPLE)
procedure POP     (S : in out STACK_TYPE,
                        T : in out STACK_PTR_TYPE,
                        SI : out STACK_ITEM_TYPE) is
begin      -- POP
      SI := S (T) ;
      T := T - 1 ;
end POP ;
```

Using the separate implementation of the procedures allows them to be written later [or to be revised] without requiring the package to be recompiled.

Note that the subprogram interface is repeated everywhere it is referenced. This ensures that the subprogram will always be referenced in the same way. If one of the interfaces is changed, an error will be reported to the user.

Chapter 7 Summary

Packages are used to collect logically related data, or data and operations. The package interface and package body may be separately compiled. Functions and procedures within the package body may also be separately compiled.

A package of data may be shared by several program units as common constants, variables, or types, but can only be used if explicitly imported by the program unit.

Packages are also used to encapsulate data objects, data types and operations which are represented as abstract, logical properties and activities, with implementation details hidden in private types or within the package body.

CHAPTER 7 QUIZ

1. What operations are allowed on private types?

2.
```
package PKG is
      type ARAY is array (INTEGER   < >  , INTEGER   < >  ) of REAL ;
      M : ARAY (1 . . 12, 8 . . 16) ;
      K : constant := 2.7514 ;
      procedure CROSS (A : in out ARAY ; X : in REAL) ;
end package PKG ;
package body PKG is separate ;

with PKG ;
procedure MAIN is

   __

begin

   __

end MAIN ;
```

Within procedure MAIN, declare a variable GRID of type ARAY with the same dimensions as M. Declare a constant TWO_K equal to 2 * K.

In the procedure, set all values of the array M to the constant TWO_K.

Call procedure CROSS with array GRID and the value in matrix M of the element in the third column and fourteenth row.

3. Rewrite procedure MAIN and include a "use clause."

1. Comparison, assignment, user defined functions

2.
```
with PKG ;
procedure MAIN is
      TWO_K : constant := 2 * PKG_K ;
      GRID : PKG . ARAY (1 . . 12, 8 . .16) ;
begin
      for I in 1 . . 12 loop
            for J in 8 . . 16 loop
                  PKG . M := TWO_K ;
            end loop ;
      end loop ;
      GRID := PKG . M ;
      CROSS (GRID, PKG . M (14, 3)) ;
end MAIN ;
```

3.
```
with PKG ;
procedure MAIN is
      use PKG ;
            TWO_K : constant := 2 * K ;
            GRID : ARAY (1 . . 12, 8 . . 16) ;
begin
      for I in 1 . . 12 loop
            for J in 8 . . 16 loop
                  M := TWO_K ;
            end loop ;
      end loop ;
      GRID := M ;
      CROSS (GRID, M (14, 3)) ;
end MAIN ;
```

8

EXCEPTIONS AND ATTRIBUTES

EXCEPTIONS AND ATTRIBUTES

A. Exceptions

Ada makes many checks during compilation of a program and eliminates many errors. However, it is certainly possible to produce a valid Ada program which will fail during execution because of a run-time violation of some attribute.

These violations are usually called errors, but they can be thought of as exceptional conditions. Ada calls them exceptions and gives the programmer the capability to anticipate and handle the events without causing termination of the program.

Some exceptions are predefined in Ada and these may also be handled by user-written routines. The programmer may also define his own exceptions and the handlers, which are executed when the exception is raised.

Exceptions are declared in the declaration part of a procedure, function, package or task along with the declarations of types, variables, procedures, constants, etc.

General Format

EXCEPTION_NAME : exception ;

The scope of the exception is the program unit in which it is declared and any units it contains. That is, if procedure PROC has declarations for an exception ERR1 and a function FN, then FN1 may raise the exception ERR1 and the exception handler in PROC will handle it.

The exception is an indication that an undesirable condition has occurred. When the program detects the condition, control is transferred to the exception handler by raising the exception.

Format

raise EXCEPTION_NAME ;

162

Example

```
procedure BIG_PROC is

      procedure PROC is
            ERR1 : exception ;            -- exception declaration
            DATA_ERR : exception ;
            - - -
            function FN returns Boolean is
            begin
            - - -
                  raise ERR1 ;
                  - - -
            end FN ;
      begin      - -  PROC
            - - -
            raise ERR1 ;                  -- the exception is raised
            - - -
            - - -
      exception                           -- this is the exception handler
            when ERR1 =>   put ("ERR1 occurred") ;
            - - -
      end PROC ;
begin           - - BIG_PROC
      - - -
      - - -                               -- exception ERR1 cannot be raised here
end BIG_PROC ;
```

User written exceptions are most often raised after some condition has been checked in an if statement or case statement. The program must check for the condition represented by the user written exception name. Built-in exceptions are detected by the system and raised automatically, although they may be raised by the programmer if necessary.

Example

```
      case DATA is
            when 1 . . 10 =>   - - - ;
            when 11 . . 20 =>   - - - ;
            when others =>   raise DATA_ERR ;
      end case ;
      - - -
      if DATA  < 0 then raise DATA_ERR ;
      - - -
      case NUM is
            when 1 . . 3 =>   - - - ;
            when 4 | 5 =>   raise ERR1 ;
            when 6 . . 9 =>   - - - ;
            when 10 =>   raise DATA_ERR ;
      end case ;
```

The part of the program which acts when the exception is raised is called the exception handler. The exception handler is included after the program in the implementation part and is preceded by the word <u>exception</u>.

After exception, there are a series of <u>when</u> clauses which specify names of exceptions, acting much like a case statement. The <u>when</u> clauses select the actions to occur when the particular exception occurs. Null is a legitimate action in an exception handler. The actions in the handler replace the actions of the remainder of the unit.

When the handler is complete, the enclosing unit is complete. If the exception handler is in a subprogram, the subprogram will return to the calling program unless the exception handler has raised another exception or has re-raised the same exception. An exception is re-raised by the statement <u>raise</u>, which is used in a clause of the exception handler statement.

Example

```
procedure PROC is
     ERR1 : exception
     - - -

begin
     - - -

     raise ERR1 ;
     - - -

exception
     when ERR1 =>   put ("ERR1 in PROC") ;
          raise ;    -- this re-raises the exception ERR1 to the
                     -- enclosing unit where another exception handler
                     -- may do something
     when OTHERS =>  - - - ;
                     -- any exception not named above is handled here
end PROC ;
```

The exception raised in the current program unit and treated in its handler is now raised in the enclosing unit. An exception handler in the enclosing unit will be used to react to the condition, again serving as the rest of the unit.

Both the scope of exceptions and re-raising of exceptions becomes a complex issue beyond the scope of the current discussion. Exceptions are discussed in greater depth in the Ada Reference Manual.

WORK   AREA

1. What is an exception?

2. What is the name of the routine written to take care of an exception?

3. What reserved word will bring this routine into use in the program?

4. What is the general format of the exception declaration?

5. The exception handler is always indicated by what reserved word?

6. In what part of the program is the exception handler placed?

CORRECT   ANSWERS

1. a violation of a rule or an error condition

2. exception handler

3. raise

4. EXCEPTION_NAME : exception

5. exception

6. implementation part

---

1. Built-in Exceptions

There are five built-in exceptions in Ada: CONSTRAINT_ERROR, NUMERIC_ERROR, SELECT_ERROR, STORAGE_ERROR and TASKING_ERROR. The exception TASKING_ERROR is used with an advanced feature and will not be discussed in this text. Additionally, seven exceptions are predefined in the INPUT_ OUTPUT and TEXT_IO packages.

a. CONSTRAINT_ERROR

In the earlier discussion of types and variables, it was mentioned that an error would occur if a variable was assigned a value which was outside its range. Similarly, a constrained array is declared with a definite range for its indices and use of an index value outside the proper index range will cause an error.

In Ada, this error is called CONSTRAINT_ERROR, an exception which will cause program termination if not explicitly handled. There are five checks made at run time which may raise CONSTRAINT_ERROR. These are ACCESS_CHECK, DISCRIMINANT_CHECK, INDEX_CHECK, LENGTH_CHECK and RANGE_CHECK. Additionally, user-written checks may raise constraint errors.

ACCESS_CHECK and DISCRIMINANT_CHECK are used on advanced features and will not be discussed here. INDEX_CHECK sees that the value of an index is within proper bounds. LENGTH_CHECK sees that the proper number of indices is used. RANGE_CHECK checks that a value of a variable is within the range declared for the type, or the range of a subtype is compatible with the type.

b. NUMERIC_ERROR

For NUMERIC_ERROR, there are two automatic checks: DIVISION_ CHECK and OVERFLOW_CHECK. DIVISION_CHECK identifies a zero divisor in the operations /[division], rem and mod. OVERFLOW_CHECK checks that the result of an arithmetic operation does not overflow [i.e., the result is too large or too small for the computer to represent. Like other built-in exceptions, NUMERIC_ ERROR may also be raised by user written checks.

c. SELECT_ERROR

The select statement is like a case statement for task entries [discussed in Chapter 9]. A SELECT_ERROR occurs when no alternative of the select statement is available and there is no else part.

d. STORAGE_ERROR

The exception STORAGE_ERROR occurs when STORAGE_CHECK reveals that no more space is available for dynamic allocation of a data item, or a task, or other program unit. This check is generally encountered in more complex programs than are currently being discussed.

WORK AREA

1. What kind of error will occur if a variable is assigned a value outside its range?

2. What are the two automatic checks for NUMERIC_ERROR?

3. What is the purpose of a SELECT_ERROR?

4. What exception occurs when there is no more space available for a particular task?

5. How many CONSTRAINT_ERROR checks are made automatically at run time?

6. Is it possible for the programmer to write error checks in addition to the automatic checks?

CORRECT ANSWERS

1. CONSTRAINT_ERROR

2. DIVISION_CHECK and OVERFLOW_CHECK

3. when there is no else and no alternative to the select statement

4. STORAGE_ERROR

5. five

6. yes

---

2. Suppressing a Check

The various checks may be suppressed by using the pragma SUPPRESS. These compiler directives do not guarantee that the corresponding exception will not be raised, since the pragma is only a recommendation and the exception could be raised in a program unit compiled separately.

Format

pragma SUPPRESS (check name [.[ON =>] name]) ;

The optional ON clause limits the suppressed check to the object named, which could be a type, variable, subprogram, etc., depending on what is appropriate for the check named.

3. Using Exceptions

The handling of exceptions is the last line of defense in a program. Defining, raising and handling an exception generally should not be a primary or often used logical path in a program. It must be remembered that the exception is associated with an error or an unexpected condition.

If a condition can be anticipated, it should be handled directly in the program. For example, a good programmer will check [or otherwise assure himself] that a divisor is not zero before a division operation is attempted.

The need for exceptions is to allow a system to continue running even when an unexpected event occurs. In a batch environment, such as a typical student submitting his program for execution and waiting for the results, if an error occurs, the program stops, error messages are printed and the program is removed from the system.

However, when the program is flying an airplane or guiding a missile to its target, the program cannot stop, print error messages and disappear because a sensor was unable to provide data at the proper time.

Even in these situations, a good programmer will do many error checks. Exception handlers are only for those situations in which the programmer overlooked the possibility of bad data.

A real time program must continue to run, so a typical exception handler will cause the action which caused the exception to be retried or ignored. In beginning programs [other than to specifically exercise the use of exceptions], exception handlers will seldom be encountered except as errors in solving problems.

WORK AREA

1. What format is used if it is desired <u>not</u> to do a particular check?

2. What usually causes an exception to occur in a program?

3. What is the basic purpose of exception handlers?

4. If a possible error condition can be anticipated, where should it be handled?

5. True or False — Error handlers should most usually be used in complex programs.

CORRECT ANSWERS

1. pragma SUPPRESS

2. an error condition

3. to keep a system running even if an error occurs

4. in the program itself

5. True

B. Attributes

Every variable in Ada must have an explicitly declared type, which has associated characteristics called attributes. These describe its size, organization and other features. Often the values of the attributes may be used in the definition of an algorithm in such a way that the program becomes less dependent on a particular value.

Attributes include the maximum and minimum values of a scalar type, the first and last index of an array, the next or preceding value of a type, the exponent of a floating point number, etc. The attirubtes may be used as constants and act as functions in programs.

Most of the type attributes are associated with numeric types, both scalar and composite [arrays] and will be the subject of discussion here. Other attributes and their definition may be found in the Language Reference Manual, along with the predefined numeric types specified in the package STANDARD.

The value of the attribute of a particular type is obtained by writing the type name, then a single quote sign ['] and finally the attribute name.

Format

TYPE_NAME ' ATTRIBUTE_NAME

In general, attributes may only appear on the right side of an assignment statement; their values may not be changed by the programmer.

Scalar types include integers, enumeration types, fixed point and floating point types. They have some common attributes and several attributes which apply only to particular types.

FIRST and LAST are common attributes. For a type declared SCALAR, SCALAR ' FIRST means the minimum value of the type. Similarly, SCALAR ' LAST means the maximum value of the type.

Examples

type declaration	type ' first	type ' last
type COUNTER is range 0 . . 199 ;	0	199
type VOWEL is ('a', 'e', 'i', 'o', 'u') ;	a	u
type MASS is digits 7 range 0.0 . . 1E10 ;	0.0	1E10
type INDEX_TYPE is INTEGER ;	—— the attributes of predefined types	
type VELOCITY is FLOAT ;	—— integer and float are implementation	
	—— dependent	

The smallest integer available for an implementation is SYSTEM . MIN_INT and the largest predefined integer is SYSTEM . MAX_INT. These are not attribute values, but constants defined in package SYSTEM.

For descrete types, there is a sequence of values between the first and last values. Except for the first and last, each value has a predecessor and a successor. Two attributes (PRED and SUCC) are used to find these values.

General Format

TYPE_NAME ' PRED (VALU)

TYPE_NAME ' SUCC (VALU)

where VALU is a value of type TYPE_NAME . VALU   may be an expression.

Examples

[using the types declared above]

VBEFORE , VAFTER : VOWEL ;
CBEFORE , CAFTER : COUNTER ;

VBEFORE := VOWEL ' PRED ('e') ;   —— the value of VBEFORE is 'a'
VAFTER := VOWEL ' SUCC ('e') ;   —— the value of VAFTER is 'i'

The following uses of SUCC and PRED result in CONSTRAINT_ERROR :

VBEFORE := VOWEL ' PRED ('a') ;   —— 'a' is the first in the list so it has
                                       —— no predecessor
VAFTER := VOWEL ' SUCC ('u') ;   —— 'u' is the last in the list so it has
                                       —— no successor

WORK   AREA

1. What is the value of CBEFORE and CAFTER ?
    a.   CBEFORE := COUNTER ' PRED (47) ;
    b.   CAFTER := COUNTER ' SUCC (47) ;

2. What will be the result of the following ?
    a.   CBEFORE := COUNTER ' PRED (0) ;
    b.   CAFTER := COUNTER ' SUCC (199) ;

171

CORRECT ANSWERS

1. a. 46
    b. 48

2. a. CONSTRAINT_ERROR   zero is the lowest, can have no
                                                    predecessor
    b. CONSTRAINT_ERROR   199 is the highest, can have no
                                                    successor

---

1. Attributes POS and VAL

The attribute POS gives the <u>position</u> of the value in the sequence from
FIRST to LAST.

General Format

TYPE_NAME ' POS (VALU) ;

When VALU is a value of TYPE_NAME, which may be an expression, the result
is of type INTEGER.

Examples

Using type VOWEL declared on the previous page, the following may be
obtained:

POSITION := VOWEL ' POS ('a') ;   —— value of POSITION is 1
POSITION := VOWEL ' POS ('e') ;   —— value of POSITION is 2
POSITION := VOWEL ' POS ('i') ;   —— value of POSITION is 3
POSITION := VOWEL ' POS ('o') ;   —— value of POSITION is 4
POSITION :- VOWEL ' POS ('u') ;   —— value of POSITION is 5

POS may be used for INTEGER types, especially for ranges which do not
begin with 0 or 1.

Examples

type PHOTI is INTEGER range 77 . . 89 ;

POSITION := PHOTI ' POS (77) ;   —— POSITION = 1
POSITION := PHOTI ' POS (79) ;   —— POSITION = 3
POSITION := PHOTI ' POS (86) ;   —— POSITION = 10
POSITION := PHOTI ' POS (89) ;   —— POSITION = 13

The attribute VAL is the converse of POS. Given an integer representing
the position in the sequence, the attribute VAL returns the value of the item in that
position.

General Format

TYPE_NAME ' VAL (INT) ;

where INT is an integer and may be an expression.

Examples

[using the type VOWEL and PHOTI declared earlier]

VALU := VOWEL ' VAL (3) ;	— VALU = 'i'
VALU := VOWEL ' VAL (5) ;	— VALUE = 'u'
VALU := VOWEL ' VAL (1) ;	— VALU = 'a'
V := PHOTI ' VAL (7) ;	— V = 83
V := PHOTI ' VAL (1) ;	— V = 77
V := PHOTI ' VAL (11) ;	— V = 87
V := PHOTI ' VAL (13) ;	— V = 89

WORK AREA

1. What is the purpose of the attribute POS?

2. What is the purpose of the attribute VAL?

3. What is the value of the following?

    a.   PHOTI ' VAL (PHOTI ' POS (79)) ;
    b.   VOWEL ' POS (VOWEL ' VAL (3)) ;
    c.   VOWEL ' VAL (PHOTI ' POS (80)) ;

CORRECT ANSWERS

1. POS gives the position of the value

2. VAL gives the value in the position

3.   a. 79
        b.   3
        c. 'o'

---

2. Fixed Point Attributes

There are five fixed point attributes: DELTA, ACTUAL_DELTA, BITS, LARGE and MACHINE_ROUNDS.

a. The DELTA attribute returns a real number which is the delta used in the type declaration.

b. ACTUAL_DELTA returns a real number representing the delta being used in the implementation for the type. ACTUAL_DELTA is at least as fine as the declared delta; it may differ with different implementations, but it will never be less fine.

c. The BITS attribute returns an integer which is the number of bits used to represent numbers of the type.

d. The attribute LARGE returns a real number which is the largest number of the fixed point type.

e. MACHINE_ROUNDS returns a true Boolean if rounding is performed when calculating values of the fixed point type.

The following examples will demonstrate each of the five attributes.

Examples

```
type DOLLAR is delta .01 range 0.0 . . 10_000 ;
D , AD , L : real ;
B : integer ;
MR : Boolean ;
```

`D := DOLLAR ' DELTA ;`	—— D has the value .01
`AD := DOLLAR ' ACTUAL_DELTA ;`	—— the value of AD is implementation
	—— dependent ; it will be .01 at most.
	—— A possible value here is .0078125
	—— which is 2^{-7} or 1/128.
`B := DOLLAR ' BITS ;`	—— Again, the value of B is implementation
	—— dependent. There are 1_000_000 values
	—— in this type, requiring a minimum of 20
	—— bits. Many machines use eight bit bytes
	—— as minimum storage increments, so 24
	—— bits is a likely value.

```
L := DOLLAR ' LARGE ;              —— L has the value 10_000
MR := DOLLAR ' MACHINE_ROUNDS ;    —— If the ACTUAL_DELTA is .0078125,
                                   —— rounding will occur and the value of
                                   —— MR is true.  If ACTUAL_DELTA
                                   —— were .01, no rounding would occur.
```

3. Floating Point Attributes

There are twelve attributes of floating point numbers. Only a few will be described here. Descriptions of the others may be found in the Ada Language Manual.

General Format

FLOAT_TYPE ' ATTRIBUTE ;

DIGITS returns an integer which is the number of digits specified in the declaration of the type.

SMALL returns a real number which is the smallest positive number of the type. LARGE returns the largest number of the type.

EMAX returns an integer which is the largest exponent value allowed for the type.

MANTISSA returns the integer value which is the number of bits used to represent the mantissa of the floating point type. The remaining floating point attributes deal with machine representation of the floating point type.

Examples

```
type SPEED is digits 8 range —9.0E5 . . 7.0E6 ;
D, M, E : INTEGER ;
S, L : REAL ;

D := SPEED 'DIGITS ;               —— the value of D is 8
M := SPEED ' MANTISSA ;            —— the value of MANTISSA is implemen-
                                   ——tation dependent and correlates to the number of
                                   ——digits required.  For this example, 32 is a likely
                                   ——value for M
E := SPEED ' EMAX ;                ——E has the value 6
S := SPEED ' SMALL ;               ——S has the value .00000001
L := SPEED ' LARGE ;               ——L has the value 7.0E6
```

WORK AREA

type ALT is digits 5 range —3.0E4 . . 6.0E7 ;

What are the values of the following ?

    a.   ALT ' SMALL   b.   ALT ' DIGITS

    c.   ALT ' EMAX   d.   ALT ' LARGE

a. .00001   b. 5
c. 7   d. 6.0E7

_____

4. Array Attributes

Array types have eight attributes, most of which describe qualities of the indices. An array must have at least one index.

General Format

ARRAY_TYPE ' ATTRIBUTE ; or
ARRAY_TYPE ' ATTRIBUTE (N) ;

where N is the number of the index. N must be a static integer expression.

There are four attribute names. If a name is used without an index number it is assumed to be the first index.
The attribute FIRST returns the value of the lower bound of the first index.
Attribute LAST returns the value of the upper bound of the first index.
LENGTH returns the number of components in the first dimension of the array.
The attribute RANGE defines a subtype consisting of the values in ARRAY_TYPE ' FIRST or ARRAY_TYPE ' LAST, using an index number after the attribute returns the appropriate information for that index.

Examples

type VOWEL is ('a', 'e', 'i', 'o', 'u') ;
type MATRIX is array (INTEGER range <   > , VOWEL) of REAL ;
        V : VOWEL ;
        MAT : MATRIX (3 . . 17, VOWEL) ;

        F, L, LN, VLN : INTEGER ;
        VF, VL, : VOWEL ;

_ _ _
_ _ _

        F := MAT ' FIRST ;   —— F = 3
        VF := MAT ' FIRST (2) ;   —— VF = 'a'

176

```
L  := MAT ' LAST ;          —— L = 17
VL  := MAT ' LAST (2) ;     —— VL = 'u'
LN  := MAT ' LENGTH ;       —— LN = 15
VLN := MAT ' LENGTH (2) ;    —— VLN = 5
```

WORK   AREA

```
type STOPLIGHT is (RED, YELLOW, GREEN) ;
type MAT is (STOPLIGHT, INTEGER range  < >) of INTEGER ;
     STOP : STOPLIGHT ;
     M : MAT (STOPLIGHT, 19 . . 23) ;
```

    a.   How many elements does array M have altogether?

    b.   What is the value of M ' LAST (2) ?

    c.   What is the value of STOP ' VAL (1) ?

    d.   What is the value of M ' FIRST (1) ?

    e.   What is the value of M ' FIRST ?

    f.   What happens in the following statement?

```
M (STOP ' VAL (2), 22) := M (M ' LAST, M ' FIRST (2)) ;
```

CORRECT ANSWERS

a.   15
b.   23
c.   red
d.   red
e.   red
f.   element M (yellow, 22) gets the value of M (green, 19)

---

5. Using Attributes

Attributes can be used to improve the abstraction of a program, particularly with arrays. To this point, it was necessary to know how many components were in each index level of the array to access all of them in a loop.

For example, if an array was declared to be eight rows and eight columns, two loops with explicit limits had to be written.

```
for I in 1 . . 8 loop
    for J in 1 . . 8 loop
        – – – MY_ARRAY (I, J) – – –
    end loop ;
end loop ;
```

If, at a later time, the declaration was to be changed to a 12 by 15 array, it would be necessary to search through the entire program to find and change the loops which reference the matrix to make sure that all the values are referenced.

This process is open to error and is very tedious. However, the attributes of arrays can be used to alleviate some of these problems, as shown in the example below.

Example

```
procedure LOOP_ARRAY is
    type MATRIX is array (INTEGER  < > , INTEGER  < > ) of REAL ;
    MAT : MATRIX (1 . . 10, 15 . . 29) ;
    – – –
begin
    for I in MAT ' RANGE (1) loop        —— this changes the first index
        for J in MAT ' RANGE (2) loop    —— this changes the second index
            – – –
            MAT (I, J) := – – –
        end loop ;
    end loop ;
    – – –
end LOOP_ARRAY ;
```

178

In procedure LOOP_ARRAY, the index range of MAT may be changed at will, yet the implementation of the loops can remain unchanged and still access every array element. The algorithm has been further extracted of details about the data upon which it operates, improving its portability and independence.

The use of MAT ' RANGE in the example is equivalent to MAT ' FIRST . . MAT ' LAST. Thus a loop could be written:

```
        for I in MAT ' FIRST . . MAT ' LAST loop
            — — —
        end loop ;
```

If, for example, MAT 'FIRST = 1, the loop could be written:

```
        for I in 1 . . MAT ' LAST loop
            — — —
        end loop ;
```

although this would be a loss in abstraction.

WORK   AREA

```
DK : constant := 1027 ;
type CTL_CHAR is (NUL, SOH, ETX, EOT, ENQ, ACK) ;
type CTL_NUM is INTEGER range 0 . . INTEGER ' LAST ;
type D3MAT is array (CTL_NUM, CTL_CHAR, INTEGER < > )

CC : CTL_CHAR ;
CN : CTL_NUM range INTEGER ' LAST / 4 . . INTEGER ' LAST ;
M3D : D3MAT (CC, CN, 1 . . DK) ;
```

    a.   How many values are in type CTL_NUM if integers use 16 bits ?

    b.   What is the range of CN ?

    c.   How many elements in array M3D ?

    d.   Write the Ada statements to increment each element of the array.

    e.   Write the Ada statements to increment only the last half of the elements in each dimension.

CORRECT ANSWERS

a. 32767

b. 8191 . . 16883

c. 6 x 8192 x 1024 = 50,331,648

d. for I in M3D'RANGE loop
    for J in M3D'RANGE (2) loop
        for K in M3D'RANGE (3) loop
            M3D (I, J, K) := M3D (I, J, K) + 1 ;
        end loop ;
    end loop ;
end loop ;

e. for I in M3D'LAST / 2 . . M3D'LAST loop
    for J in M3D'LAST (2) / 2 . . M3D'LAST (2) loop
        for K in M3D'LAST (3) / 2 . . M3D'LAST (3) loop
            M3D (I, J, K) := M3D (I, J, K) + 1 ;
        end loop ;
    end loop ;
end loop ;

Chapter 8 Summary

Error handling in Ada is accomplished by using exceptions. There are several pre-defined exceptions and the user may define others. If an error occurs, an exception is raised. If an exception handler is present, the error will be treated by this part of the program. If there is no exception handler, the program will terminate abnormally. Exceptions should be used to take care of any type of unexpected event.

Data in Ada have characteristics which may be used through attributes. Attributes allow programs to be more general and abstract.

180

```
package STK_PKG is
     STK_FULL : exception ;
     STK_EMPTY : exception ;
     type STACK is private ;
     procedure PUSH (S : in out STACK ; V : in INTEGER) ;
     procedure POP (S : in out STACK ; V : out INTEGER) ;
private
     STACK_LENGTH : constant := 25 ;
     type STACK is array (1 . . STACK_LENGTH) of INTEGER ;
end STK_PKG ;

package body STK_PKG is
     TOP : INTEGER ;
     procedure PUSH (S : in out STACK ; V : in INTEGER ) is
     begin
          if _____ then raise _____ ;
          end if ;
          TOP := TOP + 1 ;
          S (TOP) := V ;
     end PUSH ;
     procedure POP (S : in out STACK ; V : out INTEGER) is
     begin
          if _____ then raise _____ ;
          end if ;
          V := S (TOP) ;
          TOP := TOP - 1 ;
     end POP ;
begin
     TOP := 0 ;
end STK_PKG ;
```

1. If STK_FULL and STK_EMPTY imply the appropriate meanings, what condition must be present to raise which exception in the procedures PUSH and POP ?

2. Where are the exceptions handled ?

CORRECT ANSWERS

1.   procedure PUSH – – –
        begin
            if TOP = STACK_LENGTH then raise STK_FULL ;
            end if ;
        end PUSH ;
alternate : if TOP = STACK ' LAST then raise STK_FULL ;

        procedure POP – – –
        begin
            if TOP = 0 then raise STK_EMPTY ;
            end if ;
        end POP ;
alternate: if TOP < STACK ' FIRST then raise STK_EMPTY ;

2.   When an exception is defined in a package, the handler is in a program
        which uses the package.

9
ADVANCED FEATURES

ADVANCED TOPICS

A. General

Ada has many features which require sophistication and experience to understand and use. These features are generally not useful to the beginner. However, some may want to experiment with the features so brief introductions will be presented.

Complete discussions may be found in the Ada Language Reference Manual. Brief discussions are included here to suggest possible uses of these features so that students may be encouraged to seek further explanations.

B. Generics

Because of the strong use of types in Ada, the subprograms that have been used perform on only one type. If a similar action is to be accomplished for a different type, a new subprogram must be written.

This becomes a tedious process if many subprograms must be written. Ada provides the generic mechanism which allows the same subprogram to be used for many different types.

Example

Consider the function MAX which returns the largest value of the two input parameters. For integers, MAX might be written as follows:

```
function MAX (A, B : INTEGER) return INTEGER is
    MX : INTEGER ;
begin
    if A > = B then MX := A ;
    else MX := B ;
    return MX ;
end MAX ;
```

It is likely that MAX would be useful for other types as well: float, fixed point, character and user defined types. Although this example is quite short, rewriting the function [even overloading its name] would be boring work. The generic mechanism makes things easier.

Example

```
generic
    type ITEM_TYPE is private ;
function MAX (A, B : ITEM_TYPE) return ITEM_TYPE ;

function MAX (A, B : ITEM_TYPE) return ITEM_TYPE is
    MX : ITEM_TYPE ;
```

```
      begin
          if A     = B then MX := A ;
          else MX := B ;
          return MX ;
      end MAX ;
```

The pivotal element in this generic function is ITEM_TYPE. The major activity of the function works on this type, but [as it is now] nothing is known about the characteristics of ITEM_TYPE because it is PRIVATE.

To create an instance of the generic function, a type must be supplied. A usable procedure is not created until the generic declaration is <u>instantiated</u> by providing the type to be used.

An <u>instantiation</u> of the function MAX for integers would be:

function INTMAX is new MAX (INTEGER) ;

Here a function has been created called INTMAX which is a new version of the generic function MAX for integers. Similarly, functions can be instantiated for other types.

Examples

```
    function FLOAT_MAX is new MAX (FLOAT) ;

    function FIXED_MAX is new MAX (FIXED) ;

    function CHAR_MAX is new MAX (CHAR) ;

    function YOUR_MAX is new MAX (YOUR_TYPE) ;
```

The five functions that have been instantiated all use the same source text outlined in the generic declaration above.

By using a generic function, fifteen lines were required to produce five functions. If each function was written separately, thirty-five lines would have been required. For this nearly trivial example, the number of lines written have been cut by almost 60%. Of course, these savings are only available if the same operation is to be performed on many different types.

Functions, procedures and packages may all be generic. Generic packages allow groups of related functions and procedures to be grouped together to perform a more complex activity for several types of data. The mechanism and basic pattern of generic packages is the same as for functions and procedures.

As a simple example of a generic package, consider a package which sorts arrays of one dimension and of varying lengths. The element types are also different.

The package will contain type definitions which will change and generic functions and procedures. [A generic package can contain other packages although the following example does not show this.] There are two procedures SORT and EXCHANGE and a function MAX.

Example

```
generic
    LIST_LENGTH : NATURAL ;
    type ELEMENT_TYPE is private ;
package SORT_PKG is
    type LIST_TYPE is array (1 . . LIST_LENGTH) of ELEMENT_TYPE ;

    procedure SORT (L : in out LIST_TYPE,  LIST_LENGTH : NATURAL) ;
    procedure EXCHANGE (A, B : in out ELEMENT_TYPE) ;
    function MAX (X, Y : ELEMENT_TYPE) return ELEMENT_TYPE ;
end SORT_PKG ;

package body SORT_PKG is
    -- implementations of functions and procedures
    _ _ _
    _ _ _
    _ _ _
    procedure EXCHANGE (A, B : in out ELEMENT_TYPE) is
        -- the EXCHANGE swaps A and B
        -- A gets the value of B and B gets the value of A
        T : ELEMENT_TYPE ;
    begin
        T := A ;
        A := B ;
        B := T ;
    end EXCHANGE ;
    _ _ _
    _ _ _
end SORT_PKG ;
```

To instantiate a version of the generic package, the same form is used as for a procedure or function.

Example

```
        package INT_SORT is new SORT_PKG (25, INTEGER) ;
```

The package INT_SORT will use lists of 25 elements whose type is INTEGER. The procedures and function in the package will each use parameters of type integer where ELEMENT_TYPE is now indicated.

WORK AREA

1. Instantiate versions of SORT_PKG for lists of the following lengths and types:

    a. 100 REAL
    b. 1000 character
    c. K natural

2. Write a generic stack package declaration. There are two procedures PUSH and POP. The size of the stack and the type of elements stacked are to be generic. Use a simple array to implement the stack.

    Try to keep the array declaration out of the interface part of the package.

3. Describe the difference between declaration and instantiation.

CORRECT   ANSWERS

1.   a.   package REAL_SORT is new SORT_PKG (100, REAL) ;

        b.   package CHAR_SORT is new SORT_PKG (1000,
                                                 CHARACTER) ;

        c.   package NAT_SORT is new SORT_PKG (K, NATURAL) ;
                 -- the value of K must be known before
                 -- instantiation

2.

```
generic
    STACK_LENGTH : NATURAL ;
    type STACK_ITEM_TYPE is private ;
package STACK_PKG is
    procedure PUSH (NEW_ITEM : STACK_ITEM_TYPE) ;
    procedure POP (TOP_ITEM : out STACK_ITEM_TYPE) ;
end STACK_PKG ;

package body STACK_PKG is
    STACK : array (1 . . STACK_LENGTH) of STACK_ITEM_TYPE ;
    STACK_TOP : INTEGER range 0 . . STACK_LENGTH ;

    procedure PUSH (NEW_ITEM : STACK_ITEM_TYPE) ;
    begin
        STACK_TOP := STACK_TOP + 1 ;
        STACK (STACK_TOP) := NEW_ITEM ;
    end PUSH ;

    procedure POP (TOP_ITEM : out STACK_ITEM_TYPE) ;
    begin
        TOP_ITEM := STACK (STACK_TOP) ;
        STACK_TOP := STACK_TOP - 1 ;
    end POP ;
end STACK_PKG ;
```

3.   Declaration of a generic defines the algorithm and the "parameters".

      Instantiation creates a usable version from the outline provided by
         the declaration.

C. Tasking

1. Embedded Systems

Ada was originally designed to write programs for embedded computer systems. An embedded system is typically one which controls a larger system of which it is a part. Applications range from controlling the flight of missiles or airplanes, to controlling an automobile engine, to controlling a toaster or microwave oven.

The variation is enormous, but the common factor is that the system must react to stimuli immediately [in real time] rather than collect data for later analysis.

In embedded systems, a computer receives inputs from several sources [including sensors and other computers] and sends outputs to other devices and other computers.

Data is transferred either periodically or as an event occurs. Periodic data transfer can be called synchronous since an input or output is expected at a certain time or after a specific interval. Events which occur sporadically are called asynchronous since they occur at no set time or interval.

Typically, the system learns of the asynchronous event through an interrupt. An interrupt is a flag which is set when an event occurs. Interrupts may be detected by software which checks a particular part of memory frequently to see if the event has occurred.

A second type of interrupt sets a flag in the processor of the computer which causes the immediate halt of current processing and the immediate handling of the interrupt.

A hardware interrupt is usually handled by transferring control to a program waiting at a specific location in memory. Most computers have facility for only a few hardware interrupts, so these interrupts are generally reserved for the most critical events.

Ada allows the programmer to write handlers for the hardware interrupts and to put the handlers at a specific location by using the representation specification. This may be used to place a data object subprogram, package, task, or task entry at a specific location.

Example

```
task INTERRUPT_HANDLER is
    entry DONE ;
    for DONE use at 16 # 48 # ;
end ;
```

This example indicates that the interrupt DONE is handled by a routine which begins at location 48, base 16 [decimal address is 72]. The task body would describe the algorithm for the interrupt handler.

A complete explanation is beyond the scope of this text.

2. Task Structure

Another attribute of embedded systems is that there are often several computers performing duties at the same time. A system which has more than one computer is called a multiprocessor system. The computers are connected to form a network of some kind. The fact that the computers are performing simultaneously means that the system is doing parallel processing.

In Ada, the task structure supports parallel processing and multiprocessors. Tasks can be used in several general situations in which a resource must support several users. In some cases [where there are no special requirements for timing or protection of data], a package may be used. Tasks are used when synchronization is cruciai.

Suppose a particular area in memory is set aside to receive messages from any one of a number of senders. It would be quite confusing if two or more senders tried to fill the message area at the same time. One sender must be forced to wait until the other is finished. This is sometimes called mutual exclusion because when a sender is using the resource [the memory area] all others are excluded from using it.

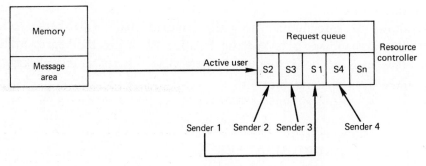

Fig. 9-1 — Resource Controller

When a sender attains control or use of the resource, other users are temporarily blocked. Typically, these requests are recorded in order and kept in the request queue.

In Ada, the resource can be represented as a task and access to it by an entry. An entry appears much like a procedure call. The only difference is that an entry call is made by a program unit outside the task and execution of the algorithm can occur in parallel with another process. The task and entry declaration are in the same lexical form as a procedure and subprogram declaration.

Example

```
procedure MAIN is
    task MESSAGE_BUFFER is
        entry FILL (MS : in MSG_TYPE) ;
        entry EMPTY (MS : out MSG_TYPE) ;
    end ;

    task body MESSAGE_BUFFER is
        - - -
        - - -

    end MESSAGE_BUFFER ;

    procedure MAIN_ACTIVITY is
        - - -
        - - -

    end ;
begin
    - - -                        -- the task is activated here
    MAIN_ACTIVITY :              -- this is a subprogram call - the task and
                                 -- the subprogram run concurrently
end MAIN ;
```

WORK   AREA

1. Define the following terms:
    a.   synchronous occurrence of events
    b.   asynchronous occurrence of events
    c.   interrupt
    d.   multiprocessor

2. For what purpose is a representation specification used?

CORRECT ANSWERS

1. a. regular occurrence
   b. sporadic occurrence
   c. a flag to notify that an asynchronous event has occurred
   d. a system that uses more than one computer

2. to place an interrupt handler into a specific location in the program.

---

3. Task Execution

After the task has been declared, it is activated by the <u>begin</u> of the enclosing compilation unit. Once it has been activated, the internal declarations of the task must be elaborated [set up in the memory and other parts of the system] and then the task begins to operate in parallel with the procedure in which the task is declared.

If there are no <u>entry</u> declarations for the task, the statements of the task are executed. If an entry is present, execution continues until the handler for the entry [in the form of an <u>accept</u> statement] is encountered. The task then waits for a call to that entry name and activity will resume when the call is received.

The entry call may be thought of as an asynchronous software interrupt, since it may occur at any time and does not cause a state change in any of the hardware interrupt indicators.

In the following example, two acts are allowed: filling the message buffer and emptying it. There is an implied sequence of events, that is, there must be something in the buffer before it can be emptied. To force the task to accept work requests in the proper order, the accept statements should be written in the order the activities are to take place.

Example

```
task body MESSAGE_BUFFER is
    BUFFER : BUFFER_TYPE ;
begin
    accept FILL (MS : in MSG_TYPE) do
        BUFFER := MS ;
    end ;
    accept EMPTY (MS : out MSG_TYPE) do
        MS := BUFFER ;
    end ;
end MESSAGE_BUFFER ;
```

192

When the task is activated, it will wait for a call to fill the buffer. When the call is received and the buffer filled, the task waits for a call to empty the buffer. When the empty call has been received and the buffer emptied, then the task terminates.

A situation where the MESSAGE_BUFFER task could be used might be represented below in a greatly simplified system.

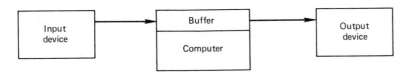

Fig. 9-2 — Simplified System

Suppose that each device [input, computer and output] is an Ada task. Each task may be active at the same time as the others, but there are certain dependencies:

1.   The input device is only allowed to fill an empty buffer [not while it is being emptied].
2.   The output device can empty only a full buffer [not while it is being filled].

It is assumed that these are the systems only activities; the computer neither fills nor empties the buffer in this example.

The input device has a message it wants to fill the buffer with 'Ada ! Sole daughter of my house and heart'. It must access the buffer through the task MESSAGE_BUFFER by making an entry call. Within the input device task will be a call which looks like:

MESSAGE_BUFFER . FILL ("Ada ! Sole daughter of my house and heart") ;

This call causes a request to be queued for the FILL entry. When the FILL entry is available, the next request on the queue is taken and the actions of the FILL entry take place. Control then passes to the EMPTY entry.

The EMPTY entry either waits for a request to be made, or takes the request at the front of the queue. The queues are First In—First Out [known as FIFO] and operate like the checkout line in a super market.

The output device makes its entry call to the MESSAGE_BUFFER task by a statement such as:

MESSAGE_BUFFER . EMPTY (PRINT_LINE) ;

where PRINT_LINE is a parameter which will take the contents of the buffer. When MESSAGE_BUFFER accepts the entry call, the contents of the buffer is transferred to

193

the parameter PRINT_LINE in the output device task. When the transfer is complete, the MESSAGE_BUFFER task terminates.

Summary

This chapter provides an introduction to two advanced topics: generics and tasking. Both of these topics are quite important, but not usually for beginning programmers. They are introduced here in the hope that some students will have their curiosity aroused and will attempt some experimentation and additional study.

CHAPTER 9 QUIZ

Note: Since a problem pertinent to this chapter is not feasible, a simple problem is provided to continue the general programming educational process. Each problem that is successfully completed by the student brings him that much closer to an understanding of the language.

Problem:

Write a program to count the words 'an', 'at', 'is', 'of', 'to', 'the' in a text. Keep the counts for the various words in an array variable called W9_CNT. Index the array with an enumeration type variable representing the words to be counted.

A procedure called GETW is used to get the words from the text. It is used by giving it a string variable in which to place the words of the text.

For example, GETW (WORD) ; would fill variable WORD with the next word of text. When the text is completely processed, the word 'XXXX' is returned to signal end—of—file. When a word other than those desired is encountered, ignore it and go on to the next word.

CORRECT ANSWER

```
procedure COUNT_WORDS is
type COMMON_WORD is (AN, AT, IS, OF, TO, THE) ;
    type WORD_COUNT is array (COMMON_WORD) of INTEGER ;
        COM_WD : COMMON_WORD ;
        WD_CNT : WORD_COUNT ;
        WORD : STRING (1 . . 10) ;
begin
        WD_CNT (AN . . THE) := 0 ;

        loop
            WORD (1 . . 10) := ' ' ;
            GETW (WORD) ;
            exit when WORD = 'XXXX' ;

            case WORD is
                when "an" =>  WD_CNT (AN) := WD_CNT (AN) + 1 ;
                when "at" =>  WD_CNT (AT) := WD_CNT (AT) + 1 ;
                when "is" =>  WD_CNT (IS) := WD_CNT (IS) + 1 ;
                when "of" =>  WD_CNT (OF) := WD_CNT (OF) + 1 ;
                when "to" =>  WD_CNT (TO) := WD_CNT (TO) + 1 ;
                when "the" =>  WD_CNT (THE) := WD_CNT (THE) + 1 ;
                when others =>   null ;
            end case ;
        end loop ;
end COUNT_WORDS ;
```

10

DEVELOPING PROGRAMS

DEVELOPING PROGRAMS

A. Five Stages of Program Creation

There are only a few motivations for using functions and procedures. Two of these are: to allow the programmer to use the same algorithm for different variables without rewriting the code and to encapsulate [to completely contain] an algorithm in a program unit.

The second reason influences the approach usually taken in program design and development. Part of the problem solution process is to identify and isolate activities sufficiently so that they may be written as a function or procedure.

The creation of a program has five stages which are really quite indistinct [Knuth, Art of Computer Programming, Vol. 1, pp. 187–188, Addison Wesley, 1973]. After being presented with a problem a vague idea of the approach to be used in solving it is formed. This is stage 1.

Nothing is very coherent or organized at this stage, because understanding of the problem is incomplete. At this stage, thinking proceeds in terms of what data is available, what data must be produced and how the transformations can be accomplished.

In stage 2, thoughts are organized into a rough outline of the proposed solution. Starting with very general descriptions of what must be done and using any descriptive method which is convenient, notes are made about what must be done.

These notes should generally reflect the flow of the future program and are often no more than sentence fragments such as: "get current speed", "calculate position", "calculate wing angle of attack", "send aileron settings", "check throttle setting", "check afterburner setting", "when afterburner on for more than 5 minuts, turn on warning light" and so on.

As thinking about the problem continues, the notes [solution sketch] takes on more and more detail and logical groupsings begin to emerge. Where similar logic is repeated, a function or procedure is defined. Sometimes it is desirable to isolate a long, complex activity in a procedure so that its logic doesn't distract from the whole problem.

For example, an activity like "calculate current position" might require several pages of program to perform. The long length of the procedure may detract from the understandability of the problem solution. Therefore, replacing these long caluclations with a procedure call "CALCULATE_POSITION" increases the readability of the main program by hiding away the irrelevant details [irrelevant to the main program] into a subprogram.

It is also very likely that other parts of the program will have to calculate the position as well. By simply assuming that a procedure will perform the position calculation, the programmer doesn't get bogged down in the details and problems of position calculation while he is concerned with determining the solution to the general problem, whatever it may be. Using suggestive procedure names allows the transformations to be represented well enough without being lost in detail so that the problem solution can continue.

This stage of the process is somewhat vaguely defined. As the solution describing process continues, a lot will change and be added as understanding of the problem increases. Whenever a part of the solution begins to grow in length and complexity, the programmer should try to fix it into a subprogram in a meaningful way.

Often, thinking of the large problem as a collection of smaller problems and then solving each of the small problems in turn in a subprogram is quite productive. One should keep breaking the problem down into smaller and smaller problems until the problem left to solve is simple.

When that much is accomplished, the programmer then backs up and tries to solve the problem at the next more complex level. This phase continues until the understanding of the problem is as complete as possible and the proposed solution has examined every part of the problem in detail.

The solution planning and design phase is the most important phase of the project. A job well done here pays off in reduced time to code, debug and test the system. The programmer should be careful not to fall into the "code mode" trap thinking that this is programming.

The job of the programmer is to produce results, not statements. Experiments have shown that programmers who spend more time planning and designing before coding have programs which have fewer statements, run faster and have much clearer logic than programs of those who immediately begin pounding away at a terminal.

It is essential to take the time to understand the problem and then to carefully plan the solution. When that is accomplished, the coding and testing will be easy.

Stage 3 of the process is to code the solution in the desired programming language. Note that this is the first time there has been any concern about what the language is to be. To this point concern has only been with the problem.

In stage 3 Ada, or Fortran, or Pascal, or any one of many other languages could be used to code the solution. Problem solution should be independent of the implementation language as far as is possible.

It is here that the programmer begins to concern himself with the details demanded by the language syntax, applying the lessons that have been learned about expressions, statements and subprograms. Learning about the problem continues in this stage as notes about the solution are transformed into a program.

In stage 4, the initial program is examined, comparing it to the solution sketch and the original problem. Often it is discovered that understanding was incomplete. In writing the program, the need for more details or processes are found to be necessary. Notes must be made in the solution sketch about what has been discovered.

Because it seems to be a natural instinct to begin coding as soon as possible, the programmer reaches this stage and realizes the need for further design. A good programmer goes back to the beginning and armed with new understanding begins the solution sketch phase again. Ideally the programmer continues this cycle of design, code, redesign until the best possible solution is produced, but practically one learns to judge that the design is good enough to implement.

Having decided that a design for the program which solves the problem has been reached, the program must then be debugged and tested. This is stage 5 of the process.

According to computer legend, the use of the term debug was literally that of removing dead insects from the hardware. The original computers built in the 1940's were very primitive devices using vacuum tubes with exposed wires for circuits. Bugs which were attracted to the glow of the vacuum tubes [like moths] were killed by the heat and fell across the circuits, shorting the wires. To get the computer running, the operators frequently had to remove the dead bugs, hence the term debugging.

Today the meaning has been extended to mean the isolation and removal of errors whether they are in the hardware or the software. The programmer is generally responsible for only software bugs.

The greatest number of errors in a new program are typographical and these are most quickly eliminated. Next, the compiler checks to see that the parts of the language are used in proper relationship to each other; this is called the syntax analysis of the program. The compiler provides information about syntax errors, which are only a small level of complexity above typographical errors as far as the ease of detection and correction is concerned.

Producing a program which has no typographical or syntax errors is easy enough, but once this state is achieved the programmer cannot consider that the program has satisfied the problem until it has been thoroughly tested.

Testing requires careful planning and design, just as developing the program does. In fact, developing the test plan should accompany the development of the program design, because the test plan should exercise every logical path in the program. The rules for testing are simple:

1. When test data is provided to the program, the programmer must know what values are expected from the program before it is executed so that an incorrect result is recognized when it occurs.
2. Enough test cases must be developed so that every logic path is exercised by the program.
3. It is important to test the boundary conditions.

For example, if part of the program is supposed to operate on the values 1 through 10, the test data should [where reasonable] force the program to use values of 0 and 1 and 10 and 11 as well as the other values.

Despite all efforts to limit the range of values expected, or describe to the user what values are allowed, somehow improper values arise and cause the program to falter or stop.

Knowing what will happen if bad data is used and being prepared for it is necessary to keep the program from stopping at a crucial time, such as when the airplane is landing or the ship is in a violent storm.

Often it is not enough to print an error report and halt; some sort of error recovery process must be included in the program. The Ada exception feature provides a good tool for error recovery.

Additionally, while the program is undergoing testing, the programmer might recognize the need to restart at an earlier stage of program design. This is not unusual, but the improved performance must be measured against the additional effort required.

However, if the difference is between a program which works correctly and one which does not, then there is no choice available. The redesign must be accomplished.

From the description of program development given here, it may be assumed [and correctly so] that programming is still an art, very much dependent on human creativity. As in other art forms, there are disciplined styles and techniques which improve the effort of the artist, but which become useful only after much practice and only when applied with diligence.

It is easy to write bad programs quickly. A mature, comprehensive piece of software is the result of careful design, development and testing.

WORK AREA

1. Developing a program is a strictly scientific procedure using a well understood sequence of steps.   True or False

2. When designing the preliminary steps of the program, careful attention is given to the details of the language features available.
   True or False

3. There are no distinct stages in program development, only levels of development based on growing understanding of the problem.
   True or False

4. The fundamental attributes of the program solution which needs to be identified are the data objects to be used, the data objects to be produced and how the data used is to be transformed to the data produced.   True or False

5. A program need only test the data values which will be most frequently used.   True or False

6. A program which compiles without syntax errors or other compiler detected errors, cannot be assumed to satisfy the problem requirements.   True or False

CORRECT ANSWERS

1. False
2. False
3. True
4. True
5. False
6. True

B. Using Functions and Procedures in Program Development

When designing the program solution to a problem, the use of functions and procedures are quite valuable. Using a descriptive function or procedure name, the program designer provides a process of unknown complexity, allowing him to think primarily about the main problem.

When the solution to the main problem is sketched out, the programmer treats each function or procedure as a new problem, developing the solution for each in terms of subprograms and statements. This process is called successive refinement, which is the breaking up of a large problem into smaller problems, each of which is easier to deal with and to solve.

Example

Consider a game that is resident on many computer systems throughout the country, called Star Trek, or Space War, or something similar. For the purpose of this example, the game description will be abridged somewhat from what is normally available.

The problem is to implement the following game:

1. As captain of the flagship [symbol E] of the space fleet, we must roam the galaxy searching out and destroying the enemy ships [symbol K].

2. We can move about or fire a space torpedo.

3. We must stay within a galaxy which is an 8 x 8 matrix.

4. Traveling within the quadrant, our ship is stopped by stars [symbol *] or by enemy ships.

5. We can only fire at enemies within the same quadrant.

6. Our ship can change quadrants, but cannot leave the galaxy.

7. When all the enemies have been destroyed, we calculate a rating by dividing the number of enemy ships at the beginning of the game by the number of commands issued.

By reading the game description through several times, it becomes obvious that it is incomplete and ambiguous [like most problem descriptions]. It presents too much detail about some things and not enough about others.

To properly understand the problem, bounds must first be put on it. In a real life problem, this is done by asking for clarification from the customer or person who posed the problem in the first place.

Often the customer is as uncertain of the requirements as the programmer. It may be necessary to have repeated meetings with the customer before both feel they understand the problem and how the software is going to contribute to the solution.

This is an application of the successive refinement principle: as more of the system becomes specified, more questions arise, which when answered allows more of the system to be specified, which leads to more questions – - - - - - -

C. Program/Project Limitations

An important part of this early process is deciding on the limits of the project. It is important that the design only includes the solution to the problem described.

In the development of large systems involving both hardware and software, there is a tendency for the hardware designer, who [because he usually has only a superficial understanding of software] asks the software designer if he can perform a particular activity. The software designer [because of a desire to appear cooperative and capable] agrees to do the function although he knows that it is nearly impossible to accomplish.

This can lead to project disaster, especially if the activity was critical to overall performance - - - and it seems to always work out that way. Thus it is important that software designers recognize their own limitations and the limitations of the programming staff, in responding to requirements realistically and based on reason rather than ego.

Part of the bounding process is to quantify requirements. Where words such as "large", "fast", or "precise" appear in the problem description, they must be replaced by numbers agreed on by both hardware and software designers as adequate and necessary. These numbers become part of the performance specification of the software which describes how fast and how large the program must be.

Other terms cannot be quantified but must be more explicitly defined before software may be designed to implement them. This will lead to refinement of the software design and specification as described previously.

D. Developing the Design Description

Examine the game description [given on page 202] to decide what must be further defined. A good approach is to try to divide the key terms into objects and activities. A good rule of thumb for identifying terms is that objects are usually nouns and activities are usually verbs. Such a division is not firm and immutable, nor will all the terms be represented by something in the program, for this is never the case in new systems.

As an exercise, re-examine the specifications for the game and devise a list of objects and activities before studying the list below.

Objects	Activities
flagship	move
galaxy	fire
enemy ship	
torpedo	
quadrant	
star	

No doubt the list developed by the reader looks different from this list. The list given here was pared back after re-reading the problem so that it appears that only essential information is listed. No matter what is on the list of the reader, it should be obvious that there is not enough information to design a program.

More must be known about the objects and the relationships they have with each other and with the activities. For example, how are quadrant and galaxy related? What is the relationship between quadrant, flagship, enemy ship, space torpedo and fire? How does the flagship move? Armed with a set of questions such as these, the software designer returns to the customer for answers.

After a lengthy discussion, more of the system takes shape. Some of the things described are depicted pictorially, others become written descriptions. To sum up the new information, a diagram [such as Fig. 10–1 on the following page] might be used as part of the design notes. Much more is known about the problem, but there is more to be added, including an orderly solution to the problem.

One important aspect of the solution has been overlooked to this point; the initial state of the system. The flagship, stars and enemies must be placed in quadrants at the start of the game. Most software systems have a "start up" routine which creates an initial state from which the operation of the system proceeds.

The player must be given certain facts at the beginning of the game:

    a.   how many enemies he must seek,
    b.   the initial position of the flagship in the quadrant and galaxy,
    c.   positions of enemies and stars

In order for the player to be able to make his decisions, the information must be displayed [an activity not explicitly called for, but necessary just the same].

At this point, a revised list of objects and activities might be as follows:

Objects	Activities
quadrant	initialize
galaxy	navigate in quadrant
flagship	navigate in galaxy
enemy-ship	fire torpedo
star	display quadrant
current position in galaxy	count commands
enemies destroyed	count enemies destroyed
enemies remaining	quit the game
commands used	

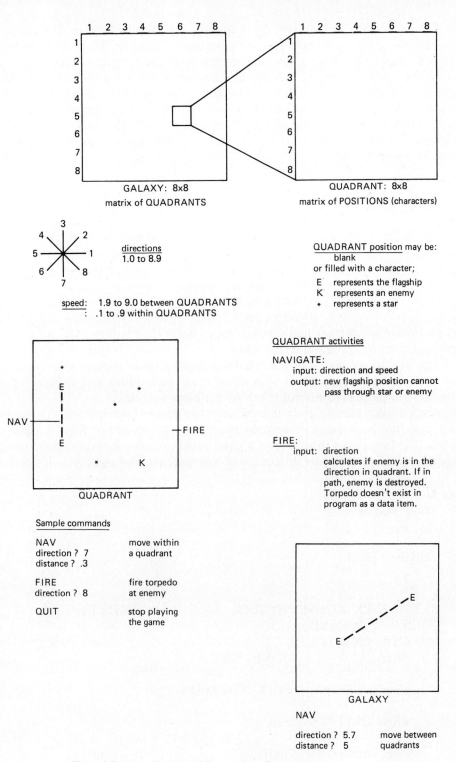

Fig. 10-1 — Design Notes for Software

205

Perception of the data and the activities involved has changed, based on additional knowledge. Also, some patterns have begun to emerge. There is perhaps enough information to begin sketching a solution, which will lead to still further questions.

In the solution sketch, related data and activities are gathered in packages which are used by the main procedure to perform the task. The main procedure determines the over-all flow of control and data in the system. In a first design sketch, few details are included. After the main procedure is described, the packages will be organized, although it is not necessary to do the design in this order if there are already existing packages to be used.

E. Techniques

There are many techniques for describing the structure of programs. Some techniques are:

> flow diagrams
> Nassi-Schneidermann charts
> program design languages
> pseudo code

Each has particular advantages and disadvantages in its detailed use, but all provide a formalized notation for program description.

The key to success is to use whatever technique is chosen consistently. The programmer should gain experience with all of these techniques and choose the method which is most compatible to his approach to problem solving.

An Ada-like pseudo code is used here for design description. A pseudo code description uses the basic form of control structures, but does not require rigorous adherence to the language syntax. It is a good technique for informal early designs, but it must be realized that pseudo code will not execute and usually will not compile.

```
procedure PLAY_GAME is
     - - main program

begin
     - - initialize game

loop
        GET_PLAYER_COMMAND (USR_CMD : out CMD_TYPE) ;
        COUNT_COMMAND ;
        case USR_CMD is
            when NAV =>    MOVE_SHIP ;

            when FIRE =>    FIRE_TORPEDO ;

            when QUIT =>    exit ;

            when others =>    null ;
        end case ;
end loop ;
end PLAY_GAME ;
```

This is the skeleton of the game. When started, an initial state is generated, then the program repeatedly looks for a command and acts on it. Thus, an activity that had not yet been considered is uncovered; getting the command from the user.

Also, it may be noted that there are many known details left out of this description, particularly what is done for the commands NAV and FIRE. At this point, it is assumed that the command-handling procedures MOVE_SHIP and FIRE_TORPEDO will contain these details.

In a similar manner, the command-handling procedures can be described using the pseudo code. Three are shown below:

procedure MOVE_SHIP is

begin

    GET_DIRECTION (D : out DIRECTION_TYPE) ;

    GET_SPEED (S : out SPEED_TYPE) ;

    if D > 1 then CHANGE_QUADRANTS
                    (D : in DIRECTION_TYPE ;
                    S : in SPEED_TYPE ;
                    P : in out POSITION) ;
    end if ;

    DISPLAY_QUADRANT (P : in POSITION) ;
end MOVE_SHIP ;

procedure FIRE_TORPEDO is
begin

    GET_DIRECTION (D : out DIRECTION_TYPE) ;

    CALCULATE_TRACK (P : in POSITION, T : out TORP_TRACK) ;

        HIT_ENEMY_CHECK (T : in TORP_TRACK,
                    HIT : out BOOLEAN) ;

    if HIT then EN_DEST := EN_DEST + 1 ;
             EN_REM := EN_REM − 1 ;
             GAME_WON_CHECK ;
             REMOVE_ENEMY ;
             DISPLAY_HIT_MESSAGE ;
             DISPLAY_QUADRANT ;

    else DISPLAY_MISS_MESSAGE ;
    end if ;

end FIRE_TORPEDO ;

```
procedure GET_PLAYER_COMMAND (USR_CMD : out CMD_TYPE) is

begin
    loop
        GET_INPUT (USR_STRNG : out USR_INPUT) ;
        case USR_STRING is
            when "NAV" =>   USR_CMD := NAV ;
                                    return ;
            when "FIRE" =>  USR_CMD := FIRE ;
                                    return ;
            when "QUIT" =>  USR_CMD := QUIT ;
                                    return ;
            when OTHERS =>   null
    end loop ;

end GET_PLAYER_COMMAND ;
```

The design of these subprograms use implemented subprograms which must be designed as well. As the design process continues, the level of detail increases with more being implemented as actions on data in simple statements [instead of procedure or function calls]. The procedures and functions called by the three procedures just described are at this low level and will not be presented here.

F. Implementation

Functions and procedures which perform a single, simple operation and do not use any other functions or procedures [except basic I/O functions] are called <u>primitives</u>. When the design completes the primitives, the system is ready to be implemented.

Before the design may be implemented, the data base must be resolved and organized into packages for use by the various procedures and functions. In this example, the few types and variables would be placed into a single package, but in a more complex system, packages would be shared by only part of the procedures.

It is necessary to associate all of the needed packages with the appropriate procedures, but not to attach unneeded packages which might inadvertently change data. While it is often very convenient to import the names of data objects employing the "use" clause, this may lead to inadvertent data alteration. For this reason, the "use" clause should be carefully considered before it is used in large systems.

Implementation of the complete design should take place from the bottom up. First, primitive procedures and functions are made to work. When the primitives are functional, the layer of the design above them may be implemented and tested.

The process continues until all of the parts of the system are implemented and tested. When each of the major subfunctions [in the given example, the activities involved in moving the ship and firing at an enemy] is known to function properly alone, then all the functions are run together as a system to make sure that they work properly together.

Only after the entire system has been debugged and totally checked out, may a programmer allow the system to become operational. Even after all of the necessary tests and checks have been accomplished, it is still more than possible that other "bugs" will show up under operational conditions and these will have to be cleaned up as they occur.

Chapter 10 Summary

The five stages of program creation are:

1. Initial ideas about the approach to problem solution are formed and organized.

2. Thoughts are organized into rough outlines, which are then broken down into small problems that are easy to solve. This is the solution planning stage.

3. The language is chosen and the language syntax is applied to the problem, developing the early efforts at the programming.

4. The initial program is compared to the solution sketch developed in stage 2. Redesign and reprogramming occurs as often as necessary.

5. The completed program is debugged and tested in small steps, moving to more complex levels until the entire program is completely clean of errors and ready to put into operation.

Functions and procedures are very useful in the design of a project and limitations must be established very early in the design stage to allow the planning to stay within reasonable limits.

There are many techniques available for describing the structure of a program. Whichever technique is chosen should be used consistently throughout the project.

Implementation should be from the bottom up. First the primitive processes are tested and made to work, followed by more complex functions until the entire program becomes error free and operational.

A
RESERVED WORD LIST

Appendix A
Ada Reserved Words

abort	declare	generic	of	select
abs	delay	goto	or	separate
accept	delta		others	subtype
access	digits		out	
all	do	if		
and		in		task
array		is	package	terminate
at	else		pragma	then
	elsif		private	type
	end	limited	procedure	
begin	entry	loop		
body	exception			use
	exit		raise	
		mod	range	
case			record	when
constant	for		rem	while
	function	new	renames	with
		not	return	
		null	reverse	
				xor

B

ASCII

AMERICAN STANDARD CODE FOR INFORMATION INTERCHANGE

Appendix B

This coded character set is to be used for the general interchange of information among information processing systems, communication systems and associated equipment.

ASCII Code

b_4	b_3	b_2	b_1	COLUMN ROW	0	1	2	3	4	5	6	7
0	0	0	0	0	NUL	DLE	SP	0	@	P	`	p
0	0	0	1	1	SOH	DC1	!	1	A	Q	a	q
0	0	1	0	2	STX	DC2	"	2	B	R	b	r
0	0	1	1	3	ETX	DC3	#	3	C	S	c	s
0	1	0	0	4	EOT	DC4	$	4	D	T	d	t
0	1	0	1	5	ENQ	NAK	%	5	E	U	e	u
0	1	1	0	6	ACK	SYN	&	6	F	V	f	v
0	1	1	1	7	BEL	ETB	'	7	G	W	g	w
1	0	0	0	8	BS	CAN	(	8	H	X	h	x
1	0	0	1	9	HT	EM	)	9	I	Y	i	y
1	0	1	0	10	LF	SUB	*	:	J	Z	j	z
1	0	1	1	11	VT	ESC	+	;	K	[	k	{
1	1	0	0	12	FF	FS	,	<	L	\	l	|
1	1	0	1	13	CR	GS	-	=	M	]	m	}
1	1	1	0	14	SO	RS	.	>	N	^	n	~
1	1	1	1	15	SI	US	/	?	O	__	o	DEL

(Column bit values: $b_7 b_6 b_5$ — col 0 = 000, col 1 = 001, col 2 = 010, col 3 = 011, col 4 = 100, col 5 = 101, col 6 = 110, col 7 = 111)

Index continued

P

packages, 138
parallel processing, 190
performance specification, 203
pop, 145, 146
pop function, 147
positional parameter passing, 133
precedence, 57
predefined type, 35
primitive, 208
private data, 150
procedure, 28, 128, 132, 198
procedure body, 28, 29
procedure call, 132
procedure interface, 28, 29
programmer defined type, 35
push, 145, 146
push procedure, 147
put, 138, 139

Q

qualifying package name, 143

R

range, 42, 46
range limits, 50
raise, 162, 163, 164
real number, 22
real time, 189
record type, 86
relational operator, 61, 62, 73
representation specification, 189
reserved words, 20

S

scaling factor, 42
separate, 158, 159
software, 8
source program, 8
stack, 145, 146

S continued

statements, 56, 68
static order, 60
stepwise refinement, 127
stored program, 5
string literal, 73
structured programming, 7, 8
stubs, 127, 157
subprogram, 126,127
subprogram call, 131
subscript, 11, 80
subtype, 39
successive refinement, 202
superscript, 25, 57
synchronous, 189, 190

T

target variable, 56
task, 190, 191, 192
truncate, 108, 112
type, 34
    array type, 80, 81, 82
    Boolean type, 36, 37
    character type, 48
    composite type, 78
    enumeration type, 48
    fixed point type, 46
    floating point type, 42
    integer type, 38
    predefined type, 35
    programmer defined type, 35
    record type, 86

U

unconstrained, 81, 82
until loop, 104
use clause, 142, 143

V

variable declaration, 34
vector, 80

W

while loop, 104
word, 67